Compact

British Columbia BIRDS

Contributors:

Wayne Campbell, Gregory Kennedy,

Krista Kagume & Carmen Adams

Lone Pine Publishing

The Publisher: Lone Pine Publishing
10145 – 81 Avenue   #5-2910 Commercial Drive
Edmonton, AB T6E 1W9   Vancouver, BC V5N 4C9

Website: www.lonepinepublishing.com

Library and Archives Canada Cataloguing in Publication

   Compact guide to British Columbia birds / contributors, Wayne Campbell ... [et al.].

   Includes bibliographical references and index.
   ISBN-13: 978-1-55105-471-1. ISBN-10: 1-55105-471-X

   1. Birds—British Columbia—Identification. 2. Bird watching—British Columbia. I. Campbell, R. Wayne (Robert Wayne), 1942-

QL685.5.B7C64 2005   598'.09711   C2005-900100-3

Editorial Director: Nancy Foulds
Project Editor: Carmen Adams
Production Manager: Gene Longson
Book Design: Curt Pillipow
Cover Design: Gerry Dotto
Cover Illustration: Gary Ross
Illustrations: Gary Ross, Ted Nordhagen, Ewa Pluciennik
Egg Photography: Alan Bibby
Layout & Production: Elliot Engley, Trina Koscielnuk
Scanning & Digital Film: Elite Lithographers Co.

We acknowledge the financial support of the Government of Canada through the Book Publishing Industry Development Program (BPIDP) for our publishing activities.

PC: 15

Contents

WATERFOWL

Snow Goose
size 107 cm • p. 18

Canada Goose
size 107 cm • p. 20

Tundra Swan
size 135 cm • p. 22

Mallard
size 61 cm • p. 24

Northern Pintail
size 63 cm • p. 26

Surf Scoter
size 36 cm • p. 28

GROUSE

Bufflehead
size 36 cm • p. 30

Ruffed Grouse
size 43 cm • p. 32

Common Loon
size 80 cm • p. 34

DIVING BIRDS

Red-necked Grebe
size 50 cm • p. 36

Sooty Shearwater
size 160 cm • p. 38

Fork-tailed Storm-Petrel
size 74 cm • p. 40

BITTERNS, HERONS & VULTURES

American White Pelican
size 160 cm • p. 42

Double-crested Cormorant
size 74 cm • p. 44

American Bittern
size 64 cm • p. 46

BIRDS OF PREY

Great Blue Heron
size 135 cm • p. 48

Turkey Vulture
size 72 cm • p. 50

Osprey
size 72 cm • p. 52

Bald Eagle
size 93 cm • p. 54

Cooper's Hawk
size 57 cm • p. 56

Red-tailed Hawk
size 57 cm • p. 58

Peregrine Falcon
size 43 cm • p. 60

Sandhill Crane
size 115 cm • p. 62

Killdeer
size 26 cm • p. 64

Black Oystercatcher
size 27 cm • p. 66

Spotted Sandpiper
size 19 cm • p. 68

Sanderling
size 19 cm • p. 70

Wilson's Snipe
size 28 cm • p. 72

Wilson's Phalarope
size 23 cm • p. 74

Bonaparte's Gull
size 49 cm • p. 76

Ring-billed Gull
size 49 cm • p. 78

Glaucous-winged Gull
size 37 cm • p. 80

Common Tern
size 37 cm • p. 82

Pigeon Guillemot
size 55 cm • p. 84

Marbled Murrelet
size 55 cm • p. 86

Tufted Puffin
size 55 cm • p. 88

PIGEONS

Rock Pigeon
size 32 cm • p. 90

Great Horned Owl
size 55 cm • p. 92

Barred Owl
size 55 cm • p. 94

OWLS

Northern Saw-whet Owl
size 21 cm • p. 96

Common Nighthawk
size 24 cm • p. 98

Rufous Hummingbird
size 24 cm • p. 100

NIGHTHAWKS & HUMMINGBIRDS

Belted Kingfisher
size 32 cm • p. 102

Downy Woodpecker
size 17 cm • p. 104

Northern Flicker
size 33 cm • p. 106

WOODPECKERS & FLICKERS

Pileated Woodpecker
size 45 cm • p. 108

Olive-sided Flycatcher
size 45 cm • p. 110

Northern Shrike
size 25 cm • p. 112

FLYCATCHERS

Warbling Vireo
size 15 cm • p. 114

Gray Jay
size 31 cm • p. 116

Steller's Jay
size 31 cm • p. 118

SHRIKES & VIREOS

American Crow
size 48 cm • p. 120

Common Raven
size 61 cm • p. 122

Horned Lark
size 18 cm • p. 124

JAYS, CROWS & RAVENS

Barn Swallow
size 18 cm • p. 126

Black-capped Chickadee
size 14 cm • p. 128

Chestnut-backed Chickadee
size 14 cm • p. 130

LARKS & SWALLOWS

Red-breasted Nuthatch
size 11 cm • p. 132

Brown Creeper
size 13 cm • p. 134

Winter Wren
size 12 cm • p. 136

CHICKADEES, WRENS & NUTHATCHES

Golden-crowned Kinglet
size 10 cm • p. 138

Mountain Bluebird
size 18 cm • p. 140

Swainson's Thrush
size 25 cm • p. 142

KINGLETS, BLUEBIRDS & THRUSHES

American Robin
size 23 cm • p. 144

Varied Thrush
size 24 cm • p. 146

European Starling
size 22 cm • p. 148

STARLINGS & WAXWINGS

Cedar Waxwing
size 18 cm • p. 150

Yellow Warbler
size 13 cm • p. 152

Yellow-rumped Warbler
size 13 cm • p. 154

WOOD-WARBLERS & TANAGERS

Common Yellowthroat
size 13 cm • p. 156

Western Tanager
size 18 cm • p. 158

Spotted Towhee
size 14 cm • p. 160

SPARROWS, TOWHEES & JUNCOS

SPARROWS, TOWHEES & JUNCOS

Chipping Sparrow
size 14 cm • p. 162

Song Sparrow
size 16 cm • p. 164

Dark-eyed Junco
size 16 cm • p. 166

BLACKBIRDS & ALLIES

Red-winged Blackbird
size 21 cm • p. 168

Western Meadowlark
size 24 cm • p. 170

Yellow-headed Blackbird
size 21 cm • p. 172

Brown-headed Cowbird
size 17 cm • p. 174

Purple Finch
size 14 cm • p. 176

Pine Siskin
size 14 cm • p. 178

FINCHLIKE BIRDS

American Goldfinch
size 14 cm • p. 180

House Sparrow
size 16 cm • p. 182

Introduction

If you have ever admired a songbird's pleasant notes, been fascinated by a soaring hawk or wondered how woodpeckers keep sawdust out of their nostrils, this book is for you. There is so much to discover about birds and their surroundings that birding is becoming one of the fastest growing hobbies. Many people find it relaxing, others enjoy its outdoor appeal, and for some, it is for the challenge of finding and listing different species. Others use birding as a way to reconnect with nature, or as an opportunity to socialize with like-minded people.

Whether you are just beginning to take an interest in birds or can already identify many species, there is always more to learn. We've highlighted both the remarkable traits and the more typical behaviours displayed by some of British Columbia's most abundant and noteworthy birds. A few live in specialized habitats, but most are common species that you have a good chance of encountering in your backyard or on a birdwatching outing.

BIRDING IN BRITISH COLUMBIA

A total of 495 bird species are found in British Columbia, of which over 400 occur on a regular basis, largely because of the ecological diversity of the province. Bordering the Pacific Ocean to the west and the Rocky Mountains to the east, British Columbia offers a variety of unsurpassed

Pigeon Guillemot

birdwatching opportunities. Bald Eagles gather at salmon runs, Turkey Vultures soar over farmlands and forests, and Great Blue Herons survey the wetlands. Many of our birds, such as the distinctive Tufted Puffin, are found nowhere else in Canada. Our coastline draws nesting sea birds during the spring and summer and myriads of waterfowl, geese, loons and grebes in winter. Some of British Columbia's birds are year-round residents, while others visit our province to breed or pass through on annual migrations.

Identifying birds in action and under varying conditions involves skill, timing and luck. The more you know about a bird—its range, preferred habitat, food preferences, habits and seasons of activity—the better your chances will be of finding it. Generally, spring and fall are the busiest birding times. Temperatures are moderate, many species of birds are on the move and male songbirds are belting out their unique courtship songs. Birds are most active in the early morning hours, except in winter when they forage throughout the day when milder temperatures prevail.

Another useful clue for correctly recognizing birds is knowledge of their habitat. Simply put, a bird's habitat is the place where it normally lives. Some birds prefer open water, some birds are found in cattail marshes, others like mature coniferous

Ruffed Grouse

forests, and still others prefer agricultural fields overgrown with tall grasses and shrubs. Habitats are just like neighbourhoods: if you associate friends with the suburb in which they live, you can easily learn to associate specific birds with their preferred habitats. Only in migration, especially during inclement weather, do some birds leave their usual habitat.

British Columbia has a long tradition of friendly, recreational birding. In general, British Columbia birders are willing to help beginners, share their knowledge and involve novices in their projects. Christmas bird counts, breeding bird surveys, nest box programs, migration monitoring and birding lectures and workshops provide a chance for birdwatchers of all levels to interact and share the splendour of birds. Bird hotlines in British Columbia provide up-to-date information on the sightings of rarities, which are often easier to locate than you might think. For more information or to participate in these projects, contact the following organizations:

BC Nature (Federation of British Columbia Naturalists)
c/o Parks Heritage Centre
1620 Mount Seymour Road
North Vancouver, BC
V7G 2R9
Phone: (604) 985-3057
Website: www.bcnature.ca

British Columbia Field Ornithologists
Box 45507
Westside RPO
Vancouver, BC V6S 2N5
Website: www.bcfo.ca

Biodiversity Centre for Wildlife Studies
Box 55053
3825 Cadboro Bay Road
Victoria, BC V8N 6L8
Phone: (250) 477-0465
Website: www.wildlifebc.org

Bird Hotlines
Vancouver (604) 737-3074
Victoria (250) 704-2555

BIRD FEEDING

Many people set up bird feeders in their backyard, especially in winter. It is possible to attract specific birds by choosing the right kind of food and style of feeder. Keep your feeder stocked through late spring, because birds have a hard time finding food before the flowers bloom and insects hatch. Contrary to popular opinion, birds do not become dependent on feeders, nor do they subsequently forget to forage naturally. Be sure to clean your feeder and the surrounding area regularly to prevent the spread of disease.

Landscaping your property with native plants is another way of providing natural foods for birds. Flocks of waxwings have a keen eye for red mountain ash berries and hummingbirds enjoy columbine flowers. The cumulative effects of "nature-scaping" urban yards can be a significant step toward habitat conservation (especially when you consider that habitat is often lost in small amounts—a seismic line is cut in one area and a highway is built in another). Many good books and web sites about attracting wildlife to your backyard are available.

Black Oystercatcher

European Starling

ABOUT THE SPECIES ACCOUNTS

This book gives detailed accounts of 83 species of birds that can be expected in British Columbia on an annual basis. The order of the birds and their common and scientific names follow the American Ornithologists' Union's *Check-list of North American Birds* (7th ed) and its supplements.

As well as showing the identifying features of the bird, each species account also attempts to bring the bird to life by describing its various plumage traits. One of the challenges of birding is that many species look different in spring and summer than they do in fall and winter. Many birds have breeding and nonbreeding plumages, and immature birds often look different from their parents. This book does not describe or illustrate all the different plumages of a species; instead, its focus is on the forms that are most likely to be seen in our area.

ID and **Other ID:** Large illustrations point out prominent field marks that will help you to identify each bird. Common, easily understood terms are used for the descriptions, rather than technical terms. Some of the most common anatomical features of birds are pointed out in the glossary illustration (p. 185).

Size: The average length of the bird's body from bill to tail, as well as wingspan, are given and are approximate measurements of the bird as it is seen in nature. The size is sometimes given as a range, because there is variation between individuals, or between males and females.

Voice: You will hear many birds, particularly songbirds, which may remain hidden from view. Memorable paraphrases of distinctive sounds will aid you in identifying a species by ear.

Status: A general comment, such as "abundant," "common," "uncommon" or "rare," is usually sufficient to describe the relative abundance of a species. Situations are bound to vary somewhat since migratory pulses, seasonal changes and centres of activity tend to concentrate or disperse birds.

Habitat: The habitats listed describe where each species is most commonly found. In most cases, it is a general description unless the bird is restricted to a specific habitat. Birds can turn up in almost any type of habitat, but they will usually be found in environments that provide the specific food, water, cover and, in some cases, nesting habitat that they need to survive.

Western Tanager

Similar Birds: Easily confused species are illustrated for each account. If you concentrate on the most relevant field marks, the subtle differences between species can be reduced to easily identifiable traits. Remember, even experienced birders can mistake one species for another. Some of the similar birds illustrated are accidentals and very rarely seen.

Nesting: In each species account, a photo of the bird's egg is provided and nest location and structure, clutch size, incubation period and parental duties are discussed. Because bird egg colours vary, egg colour descriptions may not always match the photo. Remember that birding ethics discourage the disturbance of active bird nests. If a nest is disturbed, you may drive away parents during a critical period or expose defenceless young to predators.

Range Maps: The range map for each species shows the overall range of the species in a season. Most birds will confine their annual movements to this range, although each year some birds wander beyond their traditional boundaries. The maps show summer (breeding) and winter ranges, as well as some migratory pathways—areas of the region where birds may appear while en route to nesting or winter grounds. The representations of the pathways do not distinguish high-use migration corridors from areas that are seldom used.

Range Map Symbols

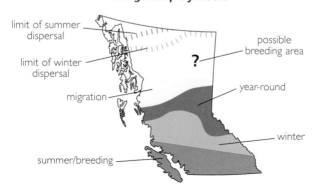

limit of summer dispersal

limit of winter dispersal

migration

summer/breeding

possible breeding area

year-round

winter

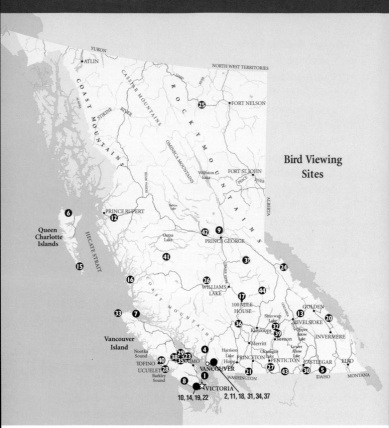

BRITISH COLUMBIA'S TOP BIRDING SITES

British Columbia is as diverse as it is large, with towering coastal rain forests, arid interior grasslands, marshy estuaries and majestic mountains. Our province can be separated into 10 major natural regions: each region is composed of a wide variety of different habitats that support a diversity of wildlife.

There are hundreds of good birding areas throughout the province. The following areas have been selected to represent a broad range of bird communities and habitats, with an emphasis on accessibility and year-round birding potential.

1. Active Pass/Gulf Islands National Park Reserve
2. Boundary Bay
3. Bowron Lake PP
4. Brackendale (Bald Eagle Reserve)
5. Creston Valley
6. Delkatla Wildlife Sanctuary (in Masset, Queen Charlotte Islands)
7. Duke of Edinburgh Ecological Reserve
8. East Sooke Regional Park
9. Eskers Provincial Park
10. Esquimalt Lagoon
11. George C. Reifel Bird Sanctuary on Delta's Reifel Island and South Arm Marshes Wildlife Management Area
12. Gitnadoiks River PP/ Lower Skeena River
13. Glacier NP
14. Goldstream Park
15. Gwaii Haanas National Park Reserve
16. Hakai Provincial Recreation Area
17. 100 Mile House (town wildlife sanctuary)
18. Iona Beach Regional Park
19. Island View Beach
20. Kootenay NP
21. Manning PP
22. Martindale Flats (Central Saanich)
23. Mitlenatch Island PP (southeast Campbell River)
24. Mount Robson PP
25. Muncho Lake PP
26. Nazko Lake PP/Chilcotin Plateau
27. Okanagan Oxbows (between Osoyoos and Oliver)
28. Pacific Rim National Park Reserve
29. Parksville-Qualicum Beach Wildlife Management Area
30. Pend d'Oreille Valley
31. Pitt-Addington Marsh/Pitt Lake
32. Salmon Arm Bay (Shuswap Lake)
33. Scott Islands
34. Serpentine Wildlife Area (Surrey)
35. Somenos marsh (near Duncan)
36. South Thompson River/ Tranquille Wildlife Management Area
37. Stanley Park (in Vancouver)
38. Strathcona PP
39. Swan Lake (north Vernon)
40. Tofino mudflats, Grice Bay
41. Tweedsmuir PP
42. Vanderhoof Bird Sanctuary
43. Vaseux Lake Migratory Bird Sanctuary
44. Wells Gray PP

PP - Provincial Park
NP - National Park

Snow Goose
Chen caerulescens

Noisy Snow Geese can be quite entertaining, creating a moving patchwork in the sky. With black wing tips and white plumage, groups of these birds appear like a dark cluster in the sky one moment and seemingly disappear the next when they synchronize their changes in flight direction. • These geese breed in the Arctic and northeastern Siberia, crossing the Bering Strait twice a year. Their smiling, serrated bills are made for grazing on short arctic tundra and gripping the slippery roots of marsh plants.

Other ID: head often stained rusty red. *Blue morph:* rare; white head and upper neck; dark blue grey body. *In flight:* black wing tips
Size: *L* 71–84 cm; *W* 1.4–1.5 m.
Voice: loud, nasal, *houk-houk* in flight, higher pitched and more constant than Canada Goose.
Status: *Coast:* common migrant and abundant in winter in the south. *Interior:* common spring and uncommon fall migrant.
Habitat: croplands, fields, estuarine marshes.

Similar Birds

Tundra Swan (p. 22)   Trumpeter Swan   Mute Swan

blue morph

dark "grin"
on bill

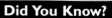

white
over all

Nesting: does not nest in B.C.; female builds
nest lined with grass, feathers and down; creamy
white eggs are 79 x 52 mm; female incubates
4–7 eggs for 22–25 days.

Did You Know?

From November through
March, while on their winter grounds in B.C., Snow
Geese spend up to 50% of
the day feeding.

Look For

Snow Geese fly in wavy,
disorganized lines, versus
the V-formation of Canada
Geese. Occasionally they
migrate together in mixed
flocks.

Canada Goose
Branta canadensis

Canada Geese mate for life and are devoted parents. Unlike most birds, the family may stay together for nearly a year, which increases the survival rate of the young. Rescuers who care for injured geese report that these birds readily adopt their human caregivers. • Wild geese can also be aggressive, especially when defending young or competing for food. Hissing sounds and low, outstretched necks are signs that you should give these birds some space. Recently, the smaller Canada Goose that breeds in Alaska, Yukon and the Northwest Territories, and winters mostly along the coast became its own species, named the "Cackling Goose."

Other ID: light brown underparts; dark brown upperparts.
Size: *L* 55–122 cm; *W* up to 1.8 m.
Voice: loud, familiar *ah-honk*.
Status: *Coast:* abundant year-round resident in the south. *Interior:* common year-round resident in the south; common migrant and breeder elsewhere.
Habitat: lakeshores, riverbanks, ponds, farmlands and city parks.

Similar Birds

Brant

Greater White-fronted Goose

long, black neck

white "chin strap"

short, black tail

white undertail coverts

Nesting: usually on the ground; occasionally in old Osprey nest; female builds a nest of grasses and plant stalks lined with down; dull white eggs are 87 x 58 mm; female incubates 3–8 eggs for 25–28 days.

Did You Know?

Of the 11 subspecies of Canada Geese described, 7 are found in B.C.

Look For

Canada Geese are found throughout B.C. on both fresh and salt water. In winter, northern inland breeders join the locals in southern areas.

Tundra Swan
Cygnus columbianus

A wave of Tundra Swans flying overhead is a sight you will never forget. They gather at staging areas in the interior, where they rest, refuel and browse on aquatic vegetation. Tundras migrating through B.C. breed in Alaska and winter mainly in the western United States. The best place to feel the stir of migration is the Creston Valley, also known as "The Valley of the Swans" in February and March and October and November.

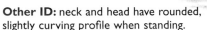

Other ID: neck and head have rounded, slightly curving profile when standing.
Size: L 1.2–1.5 m; W 2 m.
Voice: high-pitched, quivering *oo-oo-whoo* repeated in flight.
Status: *Coast:* common migrant. *Interior:* locally abundant migrant; locally abundant in winter in the south.
Habitat: shallow areas of lakes and wetlands, agricultural fields and flooded pastures.

Similar Birds

Trumpeter Swan   Mute Swan   Snow Goose (p.18)

yellow lores

neck is held
straight up

large, black bill

white plumage

Nesting: does not nest in B.C., on an island or
shoreline; nest is a large mound of vegetation;
creamy white eggs are 107 x 68 mm; female
usually incubates 4–5 eggs for 31–32 days.

Did You Know?

When Tundra Swans travel
to breeding grounds in the
high Arctic, the journey
takes over three months,
but only about 114 hours
are spent in the air.

Look For

Trumpeter Swans resemble
Tundras. Look for the yellow
lores and the straighter neck
of the Tundra compared to
the black lores and S-curved
neck of the Trumpeter.

Mallard
Anas platyrhynchos

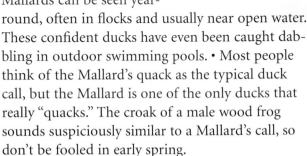

The male Mallard, with his shiny green head and chestnut brown breast, is the classic wild duck. Mallards can be seen year-round, often in flocks and usually near open water. These confident ducks have even been caught dabbling in outdoor swimming pools. • Most people think of the Mallard's quack as the typical duck call, but the Mallard is one of the only ducks that really "quacks." The croak of a male wood frog sounds suspiciously similar to a Mallard's call, so don't be fooled in early spring.

Other ID: orange feet. *Male:* grey body plumage; black tail feathers curl upward.
Size: *L* 51–71 cm; *W* 89 cm.
Voice: quacks; female is louder than male.
Status: *Coast:* common to abundant year-round. *Interior:* abundant migrant; common breeder; common in winter in the south and less common in the north.
Habitat: lakes, wetlands, rivers, city parks, agricultural areas and sewage lagoons.

Similar Birds

Northern Shoveler

American Black Duck

Common Merganser

glossy, green head

orange bill
is spattered
with black

yellow bill

chestnut brown
breast

mottled
brown overall

♂   ♀

Nesting: nest is built on the ground in grasses or under a bush; light green eggs are 58 x 41 mm; female incubates 7–10 eggs for 26–30 days.

Did You Know?

A nesting hen generates enough body heat to make the grasses around her nest grow faster. She uses them to further conceal her precious nest.

Look For

After breeding in July and August, male ducks lose their bright breeding colours. By October, most have acquired their elaborate plumage again.

Northern Pintail
Anas acuta

A long, slender neck and a long tapered tail puts this dabbling duck in a class of its own. The elegant and graceful Northern Pintail is not unique to North America. It also breeds in Asia and northern Europe.
• These early migrants begin migrating southward in mid-August, scouting out agricultural fields and wetlands. Unfortunately, this bird's choice of exposed ground nesting sites near water has resulted in a slow decline in their numbers, but staging and feeding habitat management, as well as instilling harvesting restrictions, are helping to stabilize their population.

Other ID: *Male:* chocolate brown head; dusty grey body plumage; black-and-white hindquarters.
Size: *Male: L* 64–76 cm. *Female: L* 51–56 cm.
Voice: *Male:* soft, whistling call. *Female:* rough quack.
Status: *Coast:* abundant migrant and winter resident; rare breeder. *Interior:* abundant migrant; common breeder; locally uncommon in the south in winter.
Habitat: shallow wetlands, fields and marshy lake edges.

Similar Birds

Mallard (p.24)

Gadwall

Blue-winged Teal

chocolate brown head

♂

long, slender neck

mottled, light brown overall

dark, glossy bill

♀

dusty grey body plumage

Nesting: in a small depression in vegetation; nest of grass, leaves and moss is lined with down; greenish buff eggs are 54 x 37 mm; female incubates 6–12 eggs for 22–25 days.

Did You Know?

The Northern Pintail, one of the most abundant waterfowl species on the continent, migrates at night up to 900 metres above ground.

Look For

The long pointed tail of the male Northern Pintail is easily seen in flight and points skyward when it tips up to dabble.

Surf Scoter
Melanitta perspicillata

The Surf Scoter sits like a sturdy buoy on the waves of bays, inlets and large lakes. This bird breeds in Alaska and northern Canada and is well adapted for life on rough waters, spending winters just beyond the breaking surf on the Atlantic and Pacific coasts. • Although the Surf Scoter is the only scoter that breeds and overwinters exclusively on this continent, it is largely unstudied. Much of what is known of its behaviour and distribution was documented for the first time in the latter part of the 20th century.

Other ID: sloping forehead. *Male:* black overall; orange legs. *Female:* 2 whitish patches on sides of head.
Size: L 43–53 cm; W 72–78 cm.
Voice: generally quiet; occasionally utters low, harsh croaks. *Male:* occasionally gives a low, clear whistle. *Female:* guttural *krraak krraak*.
Status: *Coast:* abundant migrant and winter visitor; locally common summer visitor. *Interior:* common migrant; uncommon summer visitor; rare in the south in winter.
Habitat: bays and inlets along the coast; large, deep lakes and slow-moving rivers in the interior.

Similar Birds

White-winged Scoter

Black Scoter

white on forehead and back of neck

large, orange bill

black spot, outlined in white, at base of bill

♂

Nesting: in a shallow scrape under bushes, near water; nest is lined with down; buff-coloured eggs are 62 x 43 mm; female incubates 5–9 eggs for 28–30 days.

Did You Know?

The Surf Scoter is often called "Skunkhead" because of the male's striking white head patches.

Look For

Huge flocks of Scoters assemble off beaches and headlands and around harbour entrances, forming a dark raft on the water.

Bufflehead

Bucephala albeola

The tiny Bufflehead might be the first diving duck you learn to identify. The striking white patch on the rear of the male's head stands out, even at a distance. • Buffleheads nest in tree cavities, using abandoned woodpecker nests or natural holes. They are small enough to squeeze into holes only 8 centimetres wide! After hatching, the ducklings remain in the nest chamber for up to three days before jumping out and tumbling to the ground.

Other ID: very small, rounded duck; short neck. *Male:* dark back. *Female:* light brown sides.
Size: *L* 33–38 cm; *W* 53 cm.
Voice: *Male:* growling call. *Female:* harsh quack.
Status: *Coast:* common migrant and winter visitor; rare breeder. *Interior:* common migrant; common breeder in the south and northeast; locally common in winter in the south; rare elsewhere.
Habitat: open water on lakes, large ponds and rivers.

Similar Birds

Hooded Merganser   Barrow's Goldeneye   Common Goldeneye

white, oval
ear patch

white wedge
on back
of head

iridescent dark green
or purple head usually
appears black

short,
grey bill

Nesting: in a tree cavity, nest is unlined or
down-filled, often near water; pale buff to
cream eggs are 51 x 37 mm; female incubates
6–12 eggs for 28–33 days.

Did You Know?

The mature female
Bufflehead returns to
the area of her birth to
search for a cavity in
which to nest.

Look For

Diving ducks' legs are set
near the back of their bodies,
so they must run along the
surface of the water to take
flight.

Ruffed Grouse
Bonasa umbellus

If you hear a loud booming echoing through the forest in early spring, you are likely listening to a male Ruffed Grouse "drumming" to announce its territory. Every spring, and occasionally in fall, the male grouse struts along a fallen log with his tail fanned and his neck feathers ruffed, beating the air periodically with accelerating wingstrokes. • In winter, featherlike scales grow out along the sides of the Ruffed Grouse's feet, creating temporary "snowshoes." Though many birds can walk on snow, only grouse and ptarmigan have this specialized feature.

Other ID: *Male:* black feathers on sides of lower neck visible when fluffed out in courtship display. *Female:* incomplete subterminal tail band.
Size: L 38–48 cm; W 56 cm.
Voice: courting male drums to produce deep, accelerating booms.
Status: common resident throughout B.C., except absent on the Queen Charlotte Is. and islands off the north coast.
Habitat: deciduous and mixed forests and riparian woodlands; favours young, second-growth stands with birch, poplar and alder with fruit-bearing shrubs.

Similar Birds

Spruce Grouse

Sharp-tailed Grouse

small, pointed head crest

grey- or reddish-barred tail has broad, dark, subterminal band and white tip

mottled, grey brown overall

♂ grey morph

Nesting: in a shallow depression on a brush pile or deadfall, often beside boulders or logs; buff-coloured eggs are 40 x 30 mm; female incubates 9–12 eggs for 23–25 days.

Did You Know?

Predation by coyotes, foxes, hawks and owls has led the Ruffed Grouse to lay larger clutches of eggs for greater chances of offspring survival.

Look For

Ruffed Grouse are easily camouflaged against the forest floor. When startled, they burst into flight, but for every grouse seen, many more go unnoticed.

Common Loon
Gavia immer

When the haunting call of the Common Loon pierces a still evening, cottagers know that summer has begun. Loons actually have many different calls. Frightened loons give a laughing distress call; separated pairs seem to wail *where aaare you?* and groups give soft, cohesive hoots as they fly.
• Common Loons are well suited to their aquatic lifestyle. Most birds have hollow bones, but loons have solid bones that reduce their buoyancy and make it easier for them to dive.

Other ID: *Nonbreeding:* duller plumage; sandy brown back; light underparts.
Size: *L* 71–89 cm; *W* 1.2–1.5 m.
Voice: alarm call is a quavering tremolo; also wails, hoots and yodels.
Status: *Coast:* common year-round resident. *Interior:* common migrant and summer visitor; uncommon in winter on ice-free lakes.
Habitat: *Breeding:* large lakes, often with islands and dense marshy area for nesting. *In winter:* bays and inlets on the coast; large lakes in the interior.

Similar Birds

Red-throated Loon

Pacific Loon

nonbreeding

green
black head

red eyes

black-and-white
"checkerboard"
upperparts

white
"necklace"

stout, thick,
black bill

breeding

white breast and
underparts

Nesting: on a muskrat pushup, small island or marshy shoreline; nest is a mound of aquatic vegetation; darkly spotted, olive brown eggs are 90 x 57 mm; both parents incubate 1–3 eggs for 24–31 days and raise young.

Did You Know?

Hungry loons will search for fish to depths of 55 metres—as deep as an Olympic-sized swimming pool is long.

Look For

In flight, the Common Loon has strong, constant wing beats with a hunch-backed appearance and legs that trail behind the tail.

Red-necked Grebe
Podiceps grisegena

nonbreeding

As evening settles over a wetland, the laughing calls of courting Red-necked Grebes signal the beginning of a new breeding season. Although Red-necked Grebes are not as vocally refined as loons, few loons can match the energy of a pair of grebes. In late May, their wild laughter often lasts through the night. • Grebes have individually webbed, or "lobed," feet. The three forward-facing toes have special flanges that are not connected to the other toes.

Other ID: *Nonbreeding:* greyish white foreneck, "chin" and "cheek."
Size: L 43–56 cm; W 61 cm.
Voice: often-repeated, laughlike, excited *ah-ooo ah-ooo ah-ooo ah-ah-ah-ah-ah.*
Status: *Coast:* abundant migrant; uncommon summer visitor; common in winter. *Interior:* common migrant and breeder; uncommon in winter in the south.
Habitat: *Breeding:* lakes with emergent vegetation, marshes, sloughs and ponds in the interior. *In winter:* bays and inlets on coast; ice-free lakes in the interior.

Similar Birds

Horned Grebe   Pied-billed Grebe   Eared Grebe

black crown

whitish "cheek"

rusty neck

straight, heavy bill
is dark above and
yellow underneath

breeding

Nesting: singly or in loose colonies; floating platform nest is built on aquatic plants or anchored
between bulrushes and cattails; white eggs, often
stained by vegetation, are 56 x 36 mm; both parents incubate 4–5 eggs for 20–23 days.

Did You Know?

It is thought that grebes
consume feathers to line
their digestive tracts,
protecting their organs
from sharp fish bones or
parasites.

Look For

Grebes feed, sleep and court
on the water. Watch for
them carrying their newly
hatched, striped young on
their backs.

Sooty Shearwater
Puffinus griseus

You may spot this bird without even venturing out to sea. The Sooty Shearwater is one of the world's most common birds. It is one of the few shearwater species that can be spotted in the waters below the surf line, where it feeds on large concentrations of schooling fish. • When our summer draws to an end, Sooty Shearwaters chase the sun back to their breeding grounds on islands in the Southern Hemisphere. • This bird shares many features with the Northern Fulmar, but has a long, slender, black bill and is more common on B.C.'s coast.

Other ID: *In flight:* silvery streak on underwing linings.
Size: *L* 41–46 cm; *W* 1.0 m.
Voice: generally silent; occasionally utters quarrelsome calls when competing for food.
Status: *Coast:* common in spring to early autumn, uncommon at other times.
Habitat: open ocean; concentrates at upwellings and current edges along the continental shelf.

Similar Birds

Northern Fulmar

Pomarine Jaeger

slender, black bill
with small "tube" on
upper mandible

dark brown body

Nesting: does not nest in B.C.; on a bare rock ledge on a cliff or on the shore of a Southern Hemisphere island; nest is made of plant material and feathers; white egg is 61 x 42 mm; pair incubates 1 egg for 52–56 days.

Did You Know?

Albatrosses, shearwaters and storm-petrels have a keen sense of smell that helps them to locate food, breeding sites and other individuals.

Look For

The Sooty Shearwater glides on its long, pointed wings in flight, flapping intermittently with rapid, deep wingbeats.

Fork-tailed Storm-Petrel

Oceanodroma furcata

The silver-tipped wings and deeply forked tail of this marine storm-petrel carries it just above the ocean's surface. The Fork-tailed Storm-Petrel more commonly appears inshore, especially when ocean temperatures rise in late summer or when westerly gales howl in late fall. • With a long incubation period and only one egg per breeding season, storm-petrels have an expensive reproductive process, so perform most of their nesting duties in the dark, out of sight of predators. The nocturnal schedule of parent Fork-tailed Storm-Petrel's involves incubation shift changes and taking turns feeding the nestling.

Other ID: pale grey underparts.
Size: L 20–23 cm; W 45 cm.
Voice: usually silent away from breeding sites; low-pitched trilling calls at the nest.
Status: *Coast:* uncommon fall migrant; abundant breeder; very rare in winter. *Interior:* very rare.
Habitat: cold, open ocean waters from near shore to beyond the continental shelf; occasionally visits bays and estuaries.

Similar Birds

Leach's Storm-Petrel

Look For

The Fork-tailed Storm-Petrel flies alongside ships when they are discarding fish oil or waste. You might also spot them snacking on a floating carcass.

bluish grey
wing tips

dark eye
patch

bluish grey
upperparts

deeply
forked tail

Nesting: colonial; on vegetated offshore islet;
self-excavated or old burrow, sometimes with
additional nest chambers; white egg is 33 x 25-mm;
pair incubates 1 egg for up to 67 days.

Did You Know?

The constant cool temperature of this bird's nesting burrow
slows the metabolism and development of the egg, allowing
parents to leave the nest unattended for days at a time.

American White Pelican
Pelecanus erythrorhynchos

This majestic wetland bird is one of only a few bird species that feeds cooperatively. A group of pelicans will herd fish into a school, then dip their bucketlike bills into the water to capture their prey. In a single scoop, a pelican can trap over 12 litres of water and fish in its bill, which is about two to three times as much as its stomach can hold. This impressive feat inspired Dixon Lanier Merritt to write: "A wonderful bird is the pelican. His bill will hold more than his belican!"

Other ID: short tail. *Breeding:* small, keeled plate develops on upper mandible; pale yellow crest on back of head.
Size: *L* 1.4–1.8 m; *W* 2.8 m.
Voice: generally quiet; rarely issues piglike grunts.
Status: *Coast:* very rare migrant and summer resident in southern regions. *Interior:* common to abundant migrant and breeder in Chilcotin-Cariboo region; non-breeding summer visitor in Creston; rare to locally common elsewhere.
Habitat: lakes; river mouths and marshes.

Similar Birds

Tundra Swan (p. 22)

Trumpeter Swan

Mute Swan

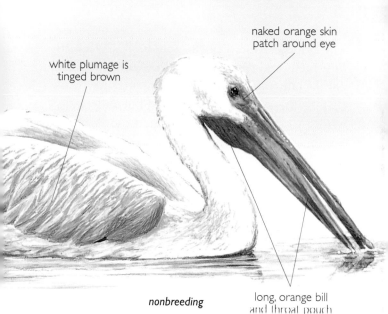

naked orange skin
patch around eye

white plumage is
tinged brown

nonbreeding

long, orange bill
and throat pouch

Nesting: colonial; on a bare, low-lying island; nest scrape is unlined or lined with twigs; dull white eggs are 87 x 56 mm; pair incubates 2 eggs for 29–36 days.

Did You Know?

The only nesting colony in B.C. is at Stum Lake in the Cariboo. Adults do not feed on their nesting lake, but forage on other lakes up to 100 km away.

Look For

When pelicans fly into the wind, they often stay close to the surface of the water. When the wind is at their backs, they will fly much higher.

Double-crested Cormorant

Phalacrocorax auritus

The Double-crested Cormorant looks like a bird but smells and swims like a fish. With a long, rudderlike tail and excellent underwater vision, this slick-feathered bird has mastered the underwater world. Most waterbirds have waterproof feathers, but the structure of the Double-crested Cormorant's feathers allows water in. "Wettable" feathers, which make this bird less buoyant, and sealed nostrils are both ideal features that make the Double-crested Cormorant an ideal diver.

Other ID: *Immature:* brown upperparts; buff throat and breast; yellowish throat patch. *In flight:* rapid wingbeats; kinked neck.
Size: L 66–81 cm; W 1.3 m.
Voice: generally quiet; may issue piglike grunts or croaks, especially near nest colonies.
Status: *Coast:* year-round resident; common on the inner south coast; uncommon on the north coast. *Interior:* increasing range; uncommon local migrant in the south; breeds at Stum L. and Creston.
Habitat: large lakes and large, meandering rivers.

Similar Birds

Common Loon (p. 34)

Pelagic Cormorant

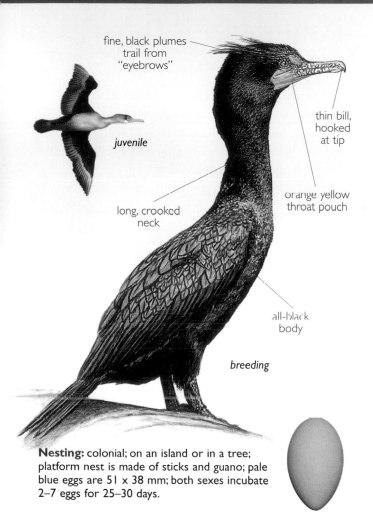

fine, black plumes trail from "eyebrows"

juvenile

thin bill, hooked at tip

orange yellow throat pouch

long, crooked neck

all-black body

breeding

Nesting: colonial; on an island or in a tree; platform nest is made of sticks and guano; pale blue eggs are 51 x 38 mm; both sexes incubate 2–7 eggs for 25–30 days.

Did You Know?

Japanese fishermen sometimes use cormorants on leashes to catch fish. This traditional method of fishing is called *Ukai*.

Look For

Double-crested Cormorants often perch on trees or piers with their wings partially spread. Lacking oil glands, they use the wind to dry their feathers.

American Bittern
Botaurus lentiginosus

The American Bittern's deep, pumping call is as common in a spring marsh as the sound of croaking frogs, but this well-camouflaged bird remains hidden. When an intruder approaches, the bittern freezes with its bill pointed skyward—its vertically streaked, brown plumage blends perfectly with the surrounding marsh. In most cases, intruders simply pass by without ever noticing the bird. An American Bittern will even adopt this reedlike position in an open field, unaware that a lack of cover betrays its presence!

Other ID: brown upperparts; brown streak from "chin" through breast; yellow legs and feet; black outer wings; dark streak from bill down neck to shoulder.
Size: *L* 59–69 cm; *W* 1.1 m.
Voice: deep, slow, resonant, repetitive *pomp-er-lunk* or *onk-a-BLONK;* most often heard in the evening or at night.
Status: *Coast:* uncommon year-round resident on the south mainland; rare resident on SE Vancouver I. *Interior:* uncommon, local breeder in Peace R. region and southward.
Habitat: brackish and freshwater wetlands and lake edges with tall, dense sedges, bulrushes or cattails.

Similar Birds

Black-crowned
Night-Heron

Green Heron

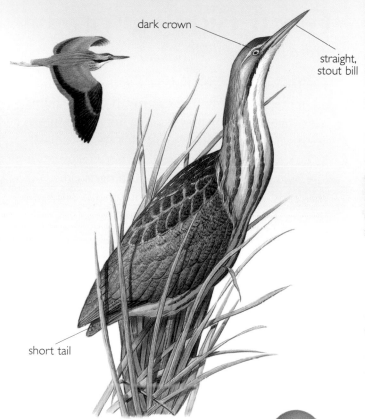

dark crown

straight,
stout bill

short tail

Nesting: in dense vegetation usually over
water; platform nest is made of sedges, cattails
and reeds; separate paths often lead to nest;
pale olive or buff eggs are 49 x 37 mm; female
incubates 3–5 eggs for 24–28 days.

Did You Know?

American Bitterns, like all
herons, have specialized
feathers that crumble into
a fine powder when the
bird preens. The powder
waterproofs other feathers.

Look For

Late mornings and early
afternoons are the best times
to hear and spot this secretive bird.

Great Blue Heron
Ardea herodias

The long-legged Great Blue Heron has a stealthy, often motionless hunting strategy. It usually hunts near water, spearing prey with its bill and swallowing it whole, but it also stalks fields and meadows in search of rodents and snakes. • Great Blue Herons settle in communal treetop nests called rookeries. Nesting herons may be sensitive to human disturbance, so observe this bird's behaviour from a safe distance.

Other ID: *Breeding:* richer colours; plumes streak from crown and throat. *In flight:* S-shaped neck; legs trail behind body; slow, steady wingbeats.
Size: *L* 1.3–1.4 m; *W* 1.8 m.
Voice: quiet away from the nest; occasional harsh *frahnk frahnk frahnk* during takeoff.
Status: *Coast:* common year-round resident in the south and uncommon in the north. *Interior:* common resident in summer; locally uncommon in winter where waters do not freeze; rare elsewhere.
Habitat: forages in the intertidal zone and along edges of rivers, lakes, marshes, fields and wet meadows.

Similar Birds

Black-crowned
Night-Heron

Sandhill Crane (p. 62)

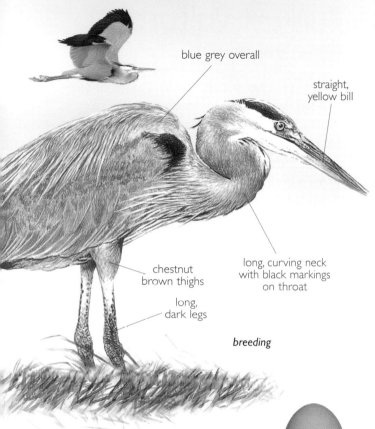

blue grey overall

straight, yellow bill

chestnut brown thighs

long, curving neck with black markings on throat

long, dark legs

breeding

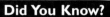

Nesting: colonial; adds to stick platform nest annually; nest width can reach 1.2 m; pale bluish green eggs are 64 x 45 mm; pair incubates 4–7 eggs for approximately 28 days.

Did You Know?

The Great Blue Heron is the tallest of all herons and egrets in North America.

Look For

In flight, the Great Blue Heron folds its neck back over its shoulders in an S-shape. Similar-looking cranes stretch their necks out when flying.

Turkey Vulture
Cathartes aura

Turkey Vultures are intelligent and social birds. Groups live and sleep together in large trees, or roosts. Some roost sites are over a century old and have been used by the same family of vultures for several generations. • Vultures have an affinity for carrion because their bills and feet are much less powerful than those of eagles, hawks or falcons, which kill live prey. The Turkey Vulture's red, featherless head may appear grotesque, but this adaptation allows the bird to stay relatively clean while feeding on messy carcasses.

Other ID: *Immature:* grey head. *In flight:* head appears small; silver grey flight feathers; black wing linings; wings are held in a shallow "V"; tips from side-to-side when soaring.
Size: L 65–80 cm; W 1.7–1.8 m.
Voice: generally silent; occasionally produces a hiss or grunt if threatened.
Status: *Coast:* common migrant and breeder along the inner south coast and Lower Mainland. *Interior:* uncommon migrant and breeder with increasing range in the far south.
Habitat: hunts over open country, transmission corridors and shorelines; nests in forests and on rocky bluffs.

Similar Birds

Golden Eagle

Bald Eagle (p. 54)

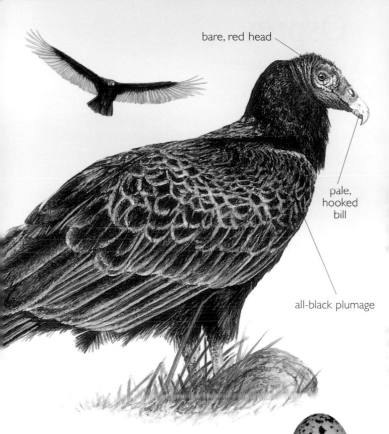

bare, red head

pale, hooked bill

all-black plumage

Nesting: in a cave, crevice, on a log or among boulders; uses no nest material; dull white eggs are 71 x 49 mm; pair incubates 2 eggs for up to 41 days.

Did You Know?

A threatened Turkey Vulture will either play dead or throw up. The odour of its vomit repulses attackers, much like the odour of a skunk's spray.

Look For

The Turkey Vulture has mastered its use of updrafts and thermals in flight. In late summer and early fall look for "kettles" of flocking vultures gathering for migration.

Osprey

Pandion haliaetus

The "Fish Hawk" is a unique member of the raptor family. With an almost exclusively fish diet, the Osprey has mastered one of the most impressive dives of the avian world. From more than 30 metres high, it dives headfirst and then rights itself and thrusts its feet forward moments before hitting the water. It emerges victorious, with prey caught in its specialized talons—two toes face forward and two face backward with spines for clamping slippery fish. • After the banning of DDT in the early 1970s, the Osprey has emerged as a true environmental success story.

Other ID: grey bill and feet. *Female:* fine, dark "necklace."
Size: *L* 56–64 cm; *W* 1.7–1.8 m.
Voice: series of melodious ascending whistles: *chewk-chewk-chewk;* also a frequent *kip-kip-kip.*
Status: *Coast:* common migrant and local breeder on south inner coast; uncommon on west Vancouver I; rare elsewhere. *Interior:* common migrant and breeder in the south becoming uncommon to rare northward.
Habitat: lakes, large wetlands and slow-moving rivers.

Similar Birds

Bald Eagle (p. 54)

Rough-legged Hawk

dark eye line

♀

all-white throat

♂

long wings extend past tail

Nesting: on a treetop, platform or atop a utility pole, usually near water; massive stick nest is reused; brown-blotched, creamy eggs are 61 x 46 mm; pair incubates 2–4 eggs for about 38 days and feeds the young for about 60 days.

Did You Know?

The Osprey is found on every continent except Antarctica, but, at one time, pesticide contamination almost extirpated them from areas of North America.

Look For

In flight, Ospreys hold their long wings in a shallow M-shape.

Bald Eagle

Haliaeetus leucocephalus

The majestic Bald Eagle is B.C.'s most versatile predator, feeding mainly on fishes and waterbirds. While soaring hundreds of metres high in the air, an eagle can spot prey swimming or feeding far below. Eagles also scavenge carrion and often steal food from other birds of prey. • Bald Eagles do not mature until their fifth or sixth year—only then will they develop the characteristic all-white head and tail plumage.

Other ID: *1st-year:* dark overall; dark bill; some white in underwings. *2nd-year:* dark "bib"; white in underwings. *3rd-year:* mostly white plumage; yellow at base of bill; yellow eyes. *4th-year:* light head with dark facial streak; variable pale-and-dark plumage; yellow bill; paler eyes. *In flight:* broad wings are held flat.
Size: *L* 76–109 cm; *W* 1.7–2.4 m.
Voice: thin, weak squeal or gull-like cackle: *kleek-kik-kik-kik* or *kah-kah-kah*.
Status: *Coast:* common breeding resident; locally abundant on fish-spawning streams. *Interior:* common migrant and breeder in the south; uncommon farther north; rare in winter near open water.
Habitat: large lakes and rivers.

Similar Birds

Golden Eagle

Osprey (p. 52)

Turkey Vulture (p. 50)

white head

yellow bill

immature

yellow feet

adult

Nesting: in a large tree; usually, but not always, near water; huge stick nest is often reused for many years; white eggs are 71 x 54 mm; pair incubates 1–3 eggs for 34–36 days.

Did You Know?

Bald Eagles mate for life and renew pair bonds by adding sticks to their nests, which can be up to 4.5 m in diameter, the largest of any North American bird.

Look For

In winter, hundreds of ducks gather on flooded fields or other ice-free waters, unknowingly providing an easy meal for hungry Bald Eagles.

Cooper's Hawk

Accipiter cooperii

A Cooper's Hawk will quickly change the scene at a backyard bird feeder when it comes looking for a meal. European Starlings, American Robins and House Sparrows are among its favourite choices of prey. • You might also spot this songbird scavenger hunting along forest edges. With the help of its short, square tail and flap-and-glide flight, it is capable of maneuvering quickly at high speeds to snatch its prey in mid-air.

Other ID: short, rounded wings; dark barring on pale undertail and underwings; blue grey back; white terminal tail band.
Size: *Male:* L 38–43 cm; W 69–81 cm.
Female: L 43–48 cm; W 81–94 cm.
Voice: fast, woodpecker-like *cac-cac-cac-cac*.
Status: *Coast:* common resident on the inner south coast; rare elsewhere. *Interior:* uncommon migrant and breeder in the south; range expanding northward to Peace River region.
Habitat: mixed woodlands, riparian woodlands, urban gardens with feeders.

Similar Birds

Sharp-shinned Hawk   American Kestrel   Merlin

squarish
head

red eyes

long, straight,
heavily barred,
rounded tail

red, horizontal
barring on
underparts

Nesting: stick nest is built in
a deciduous or coniferous tree,
often near a stream or pond;
might add to abandoned crow
nest; bluish white eggs are
49 x 38 mm; female incubates
3–5 eggs for 34–36 days; male
feeds female during incubation.

Did You Know?

Female birds of prey
are always larger than
the males. The female
Cooper's Hawk does not
hesitate to hunt birds as
large as a Rock Pigeon.

Look For

The Sharp-shinned Hawk
also occurs in B.C. and distinguishing it from the Cooper's
can be a challenge. Cooper's
Hawk is slightly larger and
has a more rounded tail tip.

Red-tailed Hawk
Buteo jamaicensis

Red-tailed Hawks are found virtually everywhere in B.C., from farmland to forest, sea level to alpine. • In warm weather, the hawks, with the help of their broad wings and tail, use thermals and updrafts to soar. These pockets of rising air provide substantial lift, which allows migrating hawks to save energy and to fly for many kilometres without flapping their wings. • Red-tails eat small mammals, medium-sized birds as well as snakes, lizards and frogs.

Other ID: *In flight:* fan-shaped tail; white or occasionally tawny brown underside and underwing linings; dark leading edge on underside of wing; light underwing flight feathers with faint barring.
Size: *Male:* L 46–58 cm; W 117–147 cm.
Female: L 51–64 cm; W 117–147 cm.
Voice: powerful, descending scream: *keeearrrr.*
Status: *Coast:* common resident on the inner south coast; uncommon resident elsewhere. *Interior:* uncommon to common resident in the south; common migrant and uncommon breeder elsewhere.
Habitat: open country with some trees; also roadsides, farm fields, rangeland and alpine.

Similar Birds

Rough-legged Hawk

Broad-winged Hawk

Swainson's Hawk

dark upperparts
with some white
highlights

dark brown band of
streaks across belly

red tail

Nesting: in mixed woodlands adjacent to open
habitat; bulky stick nest is enlarged each year;
brown-blotched, whitish eggs are 59 x 47 mm;
pair incubates 2–4 eggs for 28–35 days.

Did You Know?

The Red-tailed Hawk's
piercing call is often paired
with the image of an eagle
in TV commercials and
movies.

Look For

Some pairs arrive at their
nest sites as early as March.
Their courtship ritual
involves diving at each other,
locking talons and tumbling
towards the earth.

Peregrine Falcon

Falco peregrinus

Nothing causes more panic in a flock of ducks or shorebirds than a hunting Peregrine Falcon. This powerful raptor matches every twist and turn the flock makes, then dives to strike a lethal blow. • In the 1960s, the pesticide DDT caused peregrines to lay eggs with thin, easily breakable shells. Peregrine numbers declined dramatically until DDT was banned in North America in 1972. Since then, populations have had a steady recovery with the help of some captive-bred peregrines being introduced into cities.

Other ID: *In flight:* pointed wings; long, narrow, dark-banded tail.
Size: *Male:* L 38–43 cm; W 94–109 cm. *Female:* L 43–48 cm; W 1.1–1.2 m.
Voice: loud, harsh, continuous *cack-cack-cack-cack-cack* near the nest site.
Status: *Coast:* uncommon resident. *Interior:* rare local resident in the Okanagan Valley; rare migrant and breeder elsewhere.
Habitat: lakeshores, river valleys, river mouths and urban areas.

Similar Birds

Gyrfalcon

Merlin

prominent, dark "helmet"

blue grey back

white to buff "chin" and throat

yellow feet and cere

light underparts with dark, fine spotting and flecking

Nesting: usually on a rocky cliff or cutbank; may use a skyscraper ledge; nest site is often reused and littered with prey remains; white eggs with reddish blotches are 53 x 41 mm; pair incubates 3–5 eggs for 32–34 days.

Did You Know?

Peregrine Falcons prefer to prey on small to medium-sized seabirds, but can quickly dispatch birds as large as a Mallard.

Look For

A pair of peregrines will sometimes nest on the ledge of a tall building, right in the middle of an urban area or city.

Sandhill Crane
Grus canadensis

The Sandhill Crane's deep, rattling call can be heard long before this bird passes overhead. A coiled trachea gives this bird a vocal advantage, allowing its voice to be louder and its calls to carry farther. • At first glance, large, V-shaped flocks of Sandhill Cranes can look like flocks of Canada Geese, but the cranes often soar and circle in the air, and they do not honk like geese. • Cranes mate for life and reinforce pair bonds each spring with an elaborate courtship dance. The ritual looks much like human dancing, which may seem like a strange comparison until you witness the spectacle firsthand.

Other ID: plumage is often stained rusty red from iron oxides in water.
Size: *L* 1–1.3 m; *W* 1.8–2.1 m.
Voice: loud, resonant, rattling: *gu-rrroo gu-rrroo gurrroo.*
Status: *Coast:* uncommon migrant and local breeder. *Interior:* abundant migrant and local breeder in the south; uncommon migrant and rare breeder in the northeast; rare elsewhere.
Habitat: open ground, farm fields, lakeshores, clearcuts, marshes, wet meadows and grasslands.

Similar Birds

Great Blue Heron (p. 48)

Did You Know?

There are three subspecies of Sandhill Cranes in B.C.: one found along the coast, one in the central interior, and another in the Peace River region.

naked, red crown

long, straight bill

long neck

grey overall

Nesting: in wetlands, on a large mound of aquatic vegetation in wetlands; brown-blotched, buff eggs are 94 x 60 mm; pair incubates 2 eggs for 29–32 days; egg hatching is staggered.

Look For

The Sandhill Crane is more commonly seen in fall migration than in spring in our province. A few still breed in the Burns Bog and Pitt Meadows areas of the Lower Mainland.

Killdeer
Charadrius vociferus

The boisterous Killdeer always attracts attention. It is a gifted actor, well known for its "broken wing" distraction display. When an intruder wanders too close to its nest, it is greeted by an adult, who cries piteously while dragging a wing and stumbling about as if injured. Most predators take the bait and follow, and once the Killdeer has lured the predator far away from its nest, it miraculously recovers from the injury and flies off with a loud call.

Other ID: white face patch above bill; black forehead band; tail projects beyond wing tips. *Immature:* downy; only 1 breast band.

Size: L 23–28 cm; W 61 cm.

Voice: loud and distinctive *kill-dee kill-dee kill-deer;* variations include *deer-deer.*

Status: *Coast:* common year-round resident on the south coast; uncommon, local resident elsewhere. *Interior:* common migrant and breeder in the south and northeast regions; rare elsewhere; uncommon, local winter visitor in the south.

Habitat: open ground, fields, muddy lakeshores, sandy beaches, mudflats, gravel streambeds, wet meadows and grasslands.

Similar Birds

Semipalmated Plover

Look For

The Killdeer's nest is little more than a shallow scrape filled with speckled eggs that are camouflaged on the ground.

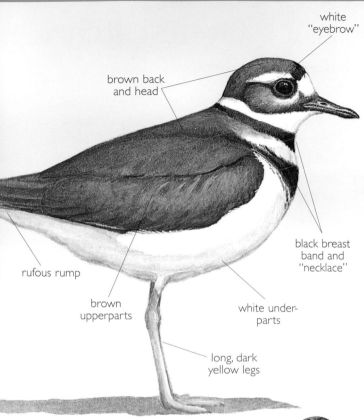

white "eyebrow"

brown back and head

rufous rump

brown upperparts

black breast band and "necklace"

white underparts

long, dark yellow legs

Nesting: on open ground, in a shallow, usually unlined depression; heavily marked, creamy buff eggs are 36 x 27 mm; pair incubates 4 eggs for 24–28 days; may raise 2 broods.

Did You Know?

In spring, you might hear a European Starling imitate the call of the vocal Killdeer.

Black Oystercatcher
Haematopus bachmani

Black Oystercatchers are devoted members of British Columbia's rocky intertidal community. They do not stray far from their rocky shoreline habitat where their meals of limpets, mussels and snails are abundant. Their flamboyant red bills are well adapted for prying open tightly sealed shells, but require practice to use. Young stay with their parents for up to a year while they perfect their foraging technique. • Ravens and crows are major predators of oystercatcher eggs and chicks.

Other ID: black head, neck and breast; brownish black elsewhere.
Size: *L* 43 cm; *W* 79 cm.
Voice: loud, piercing, repeated *wheep* or *wik* usually given in flight; series of accelerating, frantic notes with uneven trill given in spring or in territorial disputes.
Status: *Coast:* common resident, except uncommon in the Strait of Georgia.
Habitat: rocky shorelines and islands, breakwaters, jetties and reefs.

Similar Birds

American Crow (p. 120)

Common Raven (p. 122)

bright yellow eyes

orangy red eye ring

long, straight, blood red bill

sturdy, pale pink legs

Nesting: on bare ground or rocks just above the high-water mark; nest is lined with pebbles and shells; darkly marked, buff eggs are 56 x 39 mm; pair incubates 1–3 eggs for 26–28 days; young fledge at 38–40 days and are then moved to feeding sites.

Did You Know?

If the Black Oystercatcher survives the early perils of its first year, its life at the beach can be as long as 15 years!

Look For

The blood-red carrot stick bill and bright eye ring of the Black Oystercatcher are distinctive features that make it unlike any other bird in its rocky intertidal home.

Spotted Sandpiper
Actitis macularius

The Spotted Sandpiper really can call British Columbia its home. It is the only shorebird that you can expect to see almost anywhere, from sea level to the barren alpine tundra. Like a handful of other shorebirds, the female spotted sandpiper is the more aggressive partner in courtship, while the male takes care of most domestic duties in raising the family. Each summer, the female can lay up to four clutches.

Other ID: *Nonbreeding* and *immature:* pure white breast, foreneck and throat; brown bill; dull yellow legs.
Size: *L* 18–20 cm; *W* 38 cm.
Voice: sharp, crisp *eat-wheat, eat-wheat, wheat-wheat-wheat-wheat.*
Status: *Coast:* common migrant and breeder; rare in winter. *Interior:* common migrant and breeder.
Habitat: shorelines, gravel beaches, ponds, marshes, alluvial wetlands, rivers, streams, swamps, sewage lagoons and alpine.

Similar Birds

Solitary Sandpiper

Did You Know?

Sandpipers have four toes: three point forward and one points backward. Plovers, such as Killdeer, have only three toes.

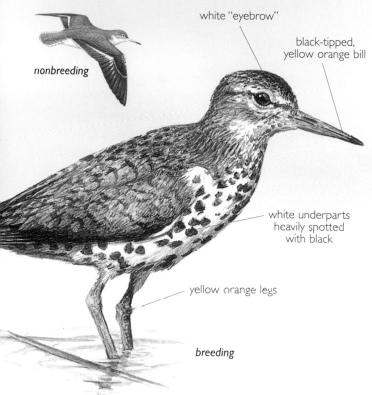

white "eyebrow"

black-tipped,
yellow orange bill

nonbreeding

white underparts
heavily spotted
with black

yellow orange legs

breeding

Nesting: usually near water; sheltered by vegetation; shallow scrape is lined with grasses; darkly blotched, creamy buff eggs are 33 x 24 mm; male incubates 4 eggs for 20–24 days and raises the young.

Look For

On shore, Spotted Sandpipers almost continuously teeter and bob their tails. When they fly across water, they stay close to its surface using very rapid, stiff, shallow wingbeats. Also, look for their white upperwing stripe in flight.

Sanderling

Calidris alba

This lucky shorebird graces sandy shorelines around the world. The Sanderling skips and plays in the waves, snatching up aquatic invertebrates before they are swept back into the water. On shores where wave action is limited, they resort to probing mudflats for a meal of small molluscs and worms. • To keep warm, Sanderlings seek the company of roosting sandpipers or plovers and turnstones. They also, occasionally, take a rest from their zigzag dance along the beach to tuck one leg up close to their body to preserve body heat.

Other ID: dark mottling on rufous head, breast and upperparts. *Nonbreeding:* pale grey upperparts; black shoulder patch (often concealed).
Size: *L* 18–22 cm; *W* 40–43 cm.
Voice: flight call is a sharp *kip* or *plick*.
Status: *Coast:* abundant migrant and winter visitor. *Interior:* rare to locally uncommon migrant.
Habitat: coastal mudflats, beaches, shorelines, spits and lagoons; inland mudflats, pond shores and wetlands.

Similar Birds

Baird's Sandpiper

Least Sandpiper

White-rumped Sandpiper

nonbreeding

relatively short,
black bill

white underparts

breeding

Nesting: does not nest in B.C.; nest is lined with grass, leaves and lichen; olive to buff eggs marked with dark brown are 36 x 25 mm; pair incubates 3–4 eggs for 24–31 days.

Did You Know?

The Sanderling is widespread, breeding across the Arctic in Alaska, Canada and Russia and wintering on every continent except Antarctica.

Look For

The latin name, *alba,* meaning "white," may describe the Sanderling's ghostly glow when it forages at night on moonlit beaches, wearing its pale, nonbreeding plumage.

Wilson's Snipe
Gallinago delicata

A courting Wilson's Snipe makes an eerie, winnowing sound, like a rapidly hooting owl. The male's specialized outer tail feathers vibrate rapidly in the air as he performs daring, headfirst dives high above a wetland. During the spring, snipes can be heard displaying day and night. • When flushed from cover, these birds perform a series of aerial zigzags to confuse predators. Because of this habit, hunters who were skilled enough to shoot snipes became known as "snipers," a term later adopted by the military.

Other ID: heavily striped neck and back; dark barring on breast, sides and flanks.
Size: *L* 27–29 cm; *W* 46 cm.
Voice: in flight, courtship song is an eerie, accelerating *woo-woo-woo-woo-woo-woo*; often sings *wheat wheat wheat* from an elevated perch; alarm call is a nasal *scaip*.
Status: *Coast:* uncommon to common resident. *Interior:* common migrant; widespread breeder; uncommon, local winter visitor.
Habitat: cattail and bulrush marshes, sedge meadows, poorly drained floodplains, bogs and fens, swamps and edges of farm fields.

Similar Birds

Short-billed Dowitcher   Long-billed Dowitcher

dark eye
stripe

heavily striped head

long, sturdy,
bicoloured bill

Nesting: usually in damp grasses; nest is made
of grasses, mosses and sometimes leaves; darkly
marked, olive buff to brown eggs are 39 × 28 mm;
female incubates 4 eggs for 18–20 days.

Did You Know?

Both parents raise the
snipe nestlings, with each
parent caring for half the
chicks.

Look For

A snipe often plunges its
entire head underwater while
probing the shallows for tasty
aquatic critters.

Wilson's Phalarope
Phalaropus tricolor

Phalaropes spin and whirl about in tight circles, stirring up aquatic insects and small crustaceans. Then, with needlelike bills, they pluck their prey from the water as it funnels toward the surface. • While incubating the eggs, the male phalarope sheds the feathers on his belly, and develops a thick skin on his underside. This "brood patch" swells with blood and provides the right temperature for incubation.

Other ID: white "eyebrow," throat and nape. *Nonbreeding:* all-grey upperparts; white "eyebrow" and grey eye line; white underparts; dark yellowish or greenish legs.
Size: *L* 22–24 cm; *W* 43 cm.
Voice: deep, grunting *work work* or *wu wu wu,* usually given on the breeding grounds.
Status: *Coast:* uncommon migrant on the inner south coast; rare, local breeder. *Interior:* common migrant and breeder in the south and southern Peace River region.
Habitat: *Breeding:* grass or sedge margins of lakes, marshes, swamps and sewage lagoons. *In migration:* shallow wetlands, ponds, marshes and sewage lagoons.

Similar Birds

Red-necked Phalarope

Red Phalarope

black eye line extends down side of neck

dark, needlelike bill

black eye line extends down side of neck and onto back

grey "cap"

♂

chestnut brown sides of neck

♀

breeding

light underparts

Nesting: often near water; well concealed in a depression lined with grasses and plant stems; brown-blotched, buff eggs are 37 x 24 mm; male incubates 4 eggs for 18–27 days and raises the young.

Did You Know?

Phalaropes are polyandrous, meaning the female mates with several males. After laying the eggs, she abandons her mate and the eggs.

Look For

Unlike most birds, the female phalarope is more colourful than the male. The male phalarope's dull colours help camouflage him while he incubates the eggs.

Bonaparte's Gull

Larus philadelphia

This gull's jet-black head gives it an appealing elegance. With its delicate plumage and behaviour, the small Bonaparte's Gull is nothing like its brash relatives. It avoids landfills, preferring to dine on insects caught in midair or plucked from the water's surface. • The Bonaparte's Gull only raises its soft, scratchy voice in excitement when it spies a school of fish or an intruder near its nest. • The phrase "black-bill Bonaparte's" is a useful memory aid for identification.

Other ID: *Nonbreeding:* white head; dark ear patch. *In flight:* white forewing wedge; black wing tips.
Size: L 30–36 cm; W 84 cm.
Voice: scratchy, soft *ear ear* while feeding.
Status: *Coast:* very abundant migrant; locally casual to rare in winter; rare to uncommon in summer. *Interior:* common to abundant migrant and breeder.
Habitat: *Breeding:* coniferous forests, bordering lakes. *In migration* and *winter:* large lakes, rivers and marine nearshore upwellings.

Similar Birds

Common Tern (p. 82)

Franklin's Gull

black head

white eye ring

nonbreeding

black bill

breeding

orange legs

Nesting: occasionally in small colonies; builds a deep nest bowl on the short, thick branches of a conifer; brown-blotched, olive to buff eggs are 52 x 36 mm; pair incubates 2–3 eggs for 24 days.

Did You Know?

This gull was named after Charles-Lucien Bonaparte, nephew of Napoleon Bonaparte and a naturalist who made significant ornithological contributions.

Look For

The Bonaparte's Gull has light buoyant flight, and in migration large flocks can be spotted plucking food from the water's surface.

Ring-billed Gull

Larus delawarensis

Few people can claim they have never seen this common and widespread gull. Highly tolerant of humans, Ring-billed Gulls are part of our everyday lives, scavenging our litter and fouling our parks. These omnivorous gulls will eat almost anything and swarm parks, beaches, golf courses and fast-food parking lots looking for food handouts, making pests of themselves. However, few species have adjusted to human development as well as the Ring-billed Gull, which is something to appreciate.

Other ID: *In flight:* black wing tips with a few white spots.
Size: *L* 46–51 cm; *W* 1.2 m.
Voice: high-pitched *kakakaka-akakaka;* also a low, laughing *yook-yook-yook.*
Status: *Coast:* common spring migrant; abundant fall migrant and nonbreeding summer visitor; uncommon in winter. *Interior:* common resident in extreme south; rare elsewhere.
Habitat: *Breeding:* bare, rocky and shrubby islands and sewage ponds. *In migration* and *winter:* lakes, rivers, landfills, golf courses, fields and parks.

Similar Birds

Herring Gull

Glaucous Gull

Thayer's Gull

white head

black ring
around bill tip

yellow eyes

pale grey
mantle

nonbreeding

yellow
bill

white
underparts

yellow legs

breeding

Nesting: colonial; in a shallow scrape on the ground lined with grasses, debris and small sticks; brown-blotched, grey to olive eggs are 59 x 42 mm; pair incubates 2–4 eggs for 23–28 days.

Did You Know?

In chaotic nesting colonies, adult Ring-billed Gulls can call out and recognize the response of their chicks.

Look For

To differentiate between gulls, look for markings on their bills and the different colours of their legs and eyes.

Glaucous-winged Gull
Larus glaucescens

Gulls can be some of the toughest birds to identify, and it often comes as a shock to beginner birders that there are no species actually named "sea-gull." The Glaucous-winged Gull is the most common gull of British Columbia. It interbreeds with the Western Gull, producing a hybrid that shares the characteristics of both birds and further complicates correctly identifying the Glaucous-winged. • This bird does not acquire its bright yellow bill until its fourth year.

Other ID: *Nonbreeding:* dingy head, neck and breast. *1st winter:* buffy white or pale brown overall with paler flight feathers; dark bill. *2nd winter:* grayish brown overall; mainly dark bill; gray mantle; white tail coverts and throat. *3rd winter:* dark-tipped pinkish bill.
Size: L 60–68 cm; W 1.4 m.
Voice: calls are a squealing *kjau,* a high-pitched, repeated *kea* and a "mewing" *ma-ah;* flight call is a single, throaty *kwoh;* attack call is *eeja-ah.*
Status: *Coast:* very common to abundant resident. *Interior:* casual to very rare visitor; several pairs breed on Okanagan L.
Habitat: saltwater and brackish bays, estuaries, harbours and open ocean; also city dumps and parks, wet fields and offshore islands.

Similar Birds

erring Gull

Western Gull

Thayer's Gull

heavy yellow bill with red spot

white head and neck

pale grey upperparts

white upper-breast

pinkish legs

breeding

Nesting: colonial and territorial; on bare rock or on the ground on island ledges; nest is made of grass, moss, roots, string, bones and seaweed; heavily-marked greenish eggs are 73 x 51 mm; pair incubates 2–4 eggs for 27–28 days.

Did You Know?

Like most gulls, this bird's diet is varied and omnivorous and includes fish, molluscs, crustaceans, nestling birds, plant material, garbage and carrion.

Look For

In flight, the Glaucous-winged Gull has grey spots on the trailing edges of its wings, near the tips.

Common Tern
Sterna hirundo

Common Terns are sleek, agile birds. They patrol the shorelines of lakes, rivers and seas during spring and fall, looking for small fishes near the surface. Although the Common Tern does not breed in British Columbia, it is the most widespread tern in North America. It spends the winter along the coasts of Central and South America.

Other ID: *Nonbreeding:* black nape; lacks black "cap."
In flight: shallow forked tail; long, pointed wings; dark grey wedge near lighter grey upperwing tips.
Size: *L* 33–41 cm; *W* 76 cm.
Voice: high-pitched, drawn-out *keee-are;* most commonly heard at colonies and in foraging flights.
Status: *Coast:* common to abundant migrant in the Strait of Georgia and Juan de Fuca Strait. *Interior:* uncommon to common local migrant in the south and Peace River region; rare elsewhere.
Habitat: large lakes, open wetlands, islands, beaches and slow-moving rivers.

Similar Birds

Forster's Tern   Arctic Tern   Caspian Tern

nonbreeding

black "cap"

black tip on red bill

red legs

white rump

breeding

Nesting: does not nest in B.C.; colonial; on an island; in a small scrape lined with pebbles, vegetation or shells; darkly blotched, creamy white eggs are 42 x 30 mm; pair incubates 1–3 eggs for 20–24 days.

Did You Know?

Terns are effortless fliers and impressive long-distance migrants: a Common Tern banded in Great Britain was recovered in Australia.

Look For

Terns hover over the water, then dive headfirst to capture small fish or aquatic invertebrates below the surface.

Pigeon Guillemot

Cepphus columba

Pigeon Guillemots are among the most widespread and commonly seen alcids along the Pacific coast. Their bright red feet and scarlet mouth lining are unmistakable. Courting birds flirt outrageously, waving their flamboyant feet, peering down each other's throats and sounding their wheezy, whistled call. • During the summer months, these seabirds forage just offshore. They dive underwater to feed, paddling quickly with their small wings and steering with their feet. Like other seabirds, guillemots must run along the water to gain enough lift for take off.

Other ID: bright red feet and mouth. *Nonbreeding:* whitish head, neck and underparts; black eye patch; mottled gray-and-white back and crown.
Size: *L* 30.5–35.5 cm; *W* 57.5 cm.
Voice: a distinctive stuttering series of wheezy notes at nest sites; silent otherwise.
Status: *Coast:* resident on the south coast; mainly breeds on the north coast.
Habitat: *Breeding:* on cliffs, in crevices or in caves on offshore islands, islets or on mainland rocky headlands; may also use old buildings, docks, wharves or piers.

Similar Birds

...cient Murrelet Marbled Murrelet (p. 86) Common Murre

slender black bill

long neck

white wing patch

black overall

breeding

Nesting: singly or in loose colonies; scrape on the ground inside a crevice or on support beams under a wharf; creamy, blotched eggs are 61 x 41 mm; pair incubates 1–2 eggs for 26–32 days.

Did You Know?

"Guillemot" is derived from the French name for William, and refers to its pigeonlike body shape and size.

Look For

Pigeon Guillemots can be spotted flashing their white wing patches among small aggregations of black birds and roosting on rocks below sea cliffs.

Marbled Murrelet
Brachyramphus marmoratus

Marbled Murrelets are one of the most unusual seabirds on the Pacific coast. These secretive birds nest deep within the mossy heights of old-growth forests but return to the ocean to feed. Each night for a month, adults bring their hungry nestlings fish from the sea, sometimes flying 70 kilometres each way. • The Marbled Murrelet's dependence on old-growth forests and coastal habitats often conflicts with human interests. Because these birds do not breed until their second year and pairs lay only one egg annually, populations are slow to recover.

Other ID: *Nonbreeding:* black "helmet"; narrow nape line, back and wings; white stripe across the scapulars, throat, and underparts.
Size: *L* 23–25 cm; *W* 40 cm.
Voice: distinctive; a piercing, loose series of high-pitched *keer* notes given both on water and in flight; whistles and groans given at the nest.
Status: *Coast:* common to abundant resident. *Interior:* very rare in spring and summer.
Habitat: ocean shorelines and harbour entrances. *Breeding:* in dense, older conifer forests, particularly coastal, old-growth Douglas-fir and Sitka spruce.

Similar Birds

Common Murre

Ancient Murrelet

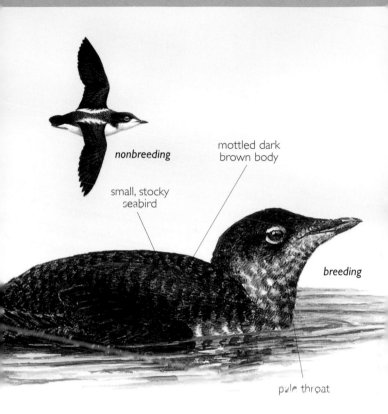

nonbreeding

small, stocky seabird

mottled dark brown body

breeding

pale throat

Nesting: solitary or semicolonial; in a shallow depression on a large limb up to 75 m high; dark-spotted, pale green egg is 61 x 38 mm; pair incubates 1 egg for 28–30 days; both parents feed the young for 27–40 days.

Did You Know?

The nesting site of the Marbled Murrelet long remained a mystery, and it took until 1990 to find a nest in British Columbia.

Look For

Marbled Murrelets fly faster and in a straighter, more direct line than most other seabirds along the west coast.

Tufted Puffin
Fratercula cirrhata

Famous for their flamboyant bills and cavalier head tufts, Tufted Puffins are an added attraction on west coast whale-watching tours. A puffin can line up more than a dozen small fish crosswise in its bill, using its round tongue and serrated upper mandible to keep the hoard in place. • Stubby wings propel alcids with surprising speed and agility underwater, but these features make for awkward take-offs and laborious flight. Weighing about 1 kilogram, puffins are almost twice as heavy as similar-sized common pigeons.

Other ID: *Nonbreeding:* large, laterally compressed, orangy bill; short, golden grey "eyebrow" tufts; all dark head and body. *Immature:* dark eyes; much smaller, all-black to yellow green bill.
Size: L 37–39 cm.
Voice: generally silent; soft growls and grunts occasionally given at nesting colony: *er-err* or *eh-errr errr errr errr.*
Status: *Coast:* locally abundant migrant and breeder along outer coast; rare in southern Strait of Georgia; winters far offshore.
Habitat: *Breeding:* on offshore islands; in soil burrows; on upwellings near islands. *Winter:* far offshore.

Similar Birds

Rhinoceros Auklet

Look For

Barkley Sound, northwest Vancouver Island, and the south end of the Queen Charlotte Islands are good places for puffin watching.

black crown and body

white face

long yellow tufts behind eyes

yellow eyes

bright red orange bill

Nesting: colonial; nest chamber is in an underground burrow up to 6 m; darkly spotted, white egg is 72 x 49 mm; pair incubates 1 egg for 41 days; both adults feed the young.

Did You Know?

Puffins depend on small fishes of a very specific size, and hundreds of these diving birds are believed to drown annually in fisherman's gill nets.

Rock Pigeon
Columba livia

Birds lack mammary glands, but the familiar Rock Pigeon, formerly known as the "Rock Dove," has an unusual feature. These birds feed their young "pigeon milk," a nutritious liquid produced in the crop. A chick inserts its bill down the adult's throat to reach the thick, protein-rich fluid. • Rock Pigeons are likely the descendants of a Eurasian bird that was first domesticated about 4500 BC. Rock Pigeons have been used as message couriers by the likes of Caesar and Napoleon, as scientific subjects and even as pets.

Other ID: colours can be blue grey, red, white or tan. *In flight:* holds wings in deep "V" while gliding.
Size: *L* 31–33 cm; *W* 71 cm.
Voice: soft, cooing *coorrr-coorrr-coorrr*.
Status: *Coast:* locally abundant at Prince Rupert and populated areas around the Strait of Georgia and Lower Mainland. *Interior:* locally common to abundant in the south near farmlands and in the southern Peace River region.
Habitat: urban areas, railway yards and agricultural areas; high cliffs often provide more natural habitat.

Similar Birds

Mourning Dove

Band-tailed Pigeon

colour is highly variable
(iridescent blue grey,
red, white or tan)

dark tipped tail

usually has
white rump

Nesting: in a barn or on a cliff, bridge or tower; in a flimsy nest of twigs, grasses and other vegetation; glossy white eggs are 39 x 29 mm; pair incubates 2 eggs for 16–19 days; may raise 2–3 broods year-round.

Did You Know?

Much of our understanding of bird migration, endocrinology, colour genetics and sensory perception comes from experiments involving this bird.

Look For

No other "wild" bird varies as much in coloration, a result of semi-domestication and extensive inbreeding over time.

Great Horned Owl
Bubo virginianus

This highly adaptable and superbly camouflaged hunter has sharp hearing and powerful vision that allows it to hunt at night as well as by day. It will swoop down from a perch onto almost any small creature that moves. • An owl has specially designed feathers on its wings: the leading edge of the first primary feather is serrated rather than smooth. This interrupts airflow over the wing and allows the owl to fly noiselessly. • Great Horned Owls begin their courtship as early as January, and by February and March, the females are already incubating their eggs.

Other ID: widely spaced "ear" tufts and beak form triangle; heavily mottled grey, brown and black upperparts.
Size: L 46–64 cm; W 91–152 cm.
Voice: breeding call is 4–6 deep hoots: *hoo-hoo-hoooo hoo-hoo* or *who's awake? me too;* male gives higher-pitched hoots.
Status: *Coast:* uncommon year-round resident; absent from the Queen Charlotte Is. *Interior:* uncommon year-round resident.
Habitat: mixed forests, fields, riparian woodlands, suburban parks and wooded edges of landfills.

Similar Birds

Long-eared Owl

Great Gray Owl

Short-eared Owl

yellow eyes

rusty orange
facial disc
is outlined
in black

white "chin"

fine, horizontal
barring on breast

Nesting: in an abandoned stick nest or in a tree cavity; adds little or no nest material; dull whitish eggs are 56 x 47 mm; mostly the female incubates 2–3 eggs for 28–35 days.

Did You Know?

The Great Horned Owl has a poor sense of smell, which might explain why it is the only consistent predator of skunks.

Look For

Owls regurgitate pellets that contain the indigestible parts of their prey. You can find these pellets, which are generally clean and dry, under frequently used perches.

Barred Owl
Strix varia

The remarkably adaptable Barred Owl arrived in British Columbia's forests in the early 1940s and has been expanding its range ever since. Found in many woodland habitats, especially those near water, the Barred now coexists with the Spotted Owl and Western Screech-Owl across southern portions of the province. • Each spring, the escalating laughs, hoots and gargling howls of Barred Owls reinforce pair bonds. They tend to be more vocal during late evening and early morning when the moon is full, the air is calm and the sky is clear.

Other ID: dark grey brown mottling on upperparts.
Size: *L* 43–61 cm; *W* 1.0–1.3 m (female is slightly larger).
Voice: loud, hooting, rhythmic call is heard mostly in spring: *Who cooks for you? Who cooks for you all?*
Status: *Coast:* common year-round resident on inner south coast; uncommon resident on Lower Mainland coast. *Interior:* uncommon year-round resident across the south and north to southern Peace River region.
Habitat: mature coniferous and mixed-wood forests, especially in dense stands near swamps, streams and lakes.

Similar Birds

| Spotted Owl | Northern Hawk Owl | Great Horned Owl (p. 92) | Great Gray Owl |

dark eyes

no "ear" tufts

horizontal barring around neck and upper breast

light-coloured bill

vertical streaking on belly

Nesting: in a natural tree cavity or abandoned stick nest; adds very little material; female incubates 2–3 white eggs for 28–33 days; male feeds the incubating female.

Did You Know?

In darkness, the Barred Owl's eyesight may be 100 times that of humans, and it is able to locate and follow prey using sound alone.

Look For

Dark eyes make the Barred Owl unique—most familiar large owls in North America have yellow eyes.

Northern Saw-whet Owl

Aegolius acadicus

The tiny Northern Saw-whet Owl makes the most of every hunting opportunity. When temperatures fall below freezing and prey is abundant, the Northern Saw-whet will catch more than it can eat, storing the extra food in trees and leaving it to freeze. Should hunting efforts fail, the owl will "incubate" its frozen cache as if it were a clutch of eggs! The Northern Saw-whet's favourite foods include mice, voles, large insects and small songbirds.

Other ID: white-spotted, brown upperparts.
Juvenile: white patch between eyes; rich brown head and breast; buff brown belly.
Size: *L* 18–23 cm; *W* 43–55 cm.
Voice: whistled, evenly spaced *whew-whew,* repeated about 100 times per minute.
Status: *Coast:* uncommon year-round resident on Queen Charlotte Is. and around Strait of Georgia; rare elsewhere. *Interior:* uncommon year-round resident south of Prince George and in southern Peace River; rare elsewhere.
Habitat: mixed coniferous and deciduous forests and wetlands at lower elevations.

Similar Birds

Boreal Owl

Northern Pygmy-Owl

Western Screech-Owl

pale, unbordered facial disc

large, rounded head

white-streaked forehead

vertical, rusty streaks on underparts

small body

short tail

Nesting: in a natural tree hollow or a nest box; white eggs are 30 x 25 mm; female incubates 5–6 eggs for 27–29 days; male feeds the female during incubation.

Did You Know?

This owl's name refers to its call, which sounds like a saw blade being sharpened, or the "bleeping" sound of a vehicle reversing.

Look For

A good way to detect the Northern Saw-whet Owl is by looking for "whitewash," or buildups of excrement, under possible roosting sites.

Common Nighthawk
Chordeiles minor

The Common Nighthawk may impress you as well as his potential mate in a unique courtship display. The male makes an energetic dive, then swerves skyward, making a hollow *boom* with his wings. • Like other members of the nightjar family, the Common Nighthawk has adapted to catch insects in midair: its beak is surrounded by feather shafts that funnel insects into its mouth. A nighthawk can eat over 2600 insects, including mosquitoes, blackflies and flying ants, in one day.

Other ID: *In flight:* bold, white "wrist" on long, pointed wings; shallowly forked, barred tail; erratic flight.
Size: *L* 22–25 cm; *W* 61 cm.
Voice: frequently repeated, nasal *peent peent;* wings make a deep, hollow *boom* during courtship dive.
Status: *Coast:* uncommon breeder on Vancouver I. and south; locally abundant in fall. *Interior:* uncommon breeder throughout; locally common in fall migration.
Habitat: *Breeding:* large forest openings, burns, clearcuts, rocky outcroppings and gravel rooftops. *In migration:* often near water; or areas with large numbers of flying insects.

Similar Birds

Common Poorwill

Look For

With their short legs and tiny feet, nighthawks sit lengthwise on tree branches and blend in perfectly with the bark.

white throat
on male

cryptic, mottled
plumage

barred underparts

Nesting: on bare ground; no nest is built; heavily marked, creamy white to buff eggs are 30 x 22 mm; female incubates 2 eggs for about 19 days; both adults feed the young.

Did You Know?

It was once believed that members of the nightjar, or "goat-sucker," family could suck milk from the udders of goats, causing the goats to go blind!

Rufous Hummingbird
Selasphorus rufus

The tiny Rufous Hummingbird is a delicate avian jewel, but its beauty hides a relentless mean streak. Sit patiently in a flower-filled meadow or alongside a hummingbird feeder, and you'll soon notice the aggressive nature of these feisty birds. They buzz past one another and chase rivals for some distance.
• Hummingbirds are among the few birds that are able to fly vertically and in reverse. In forward flight, they beat their wings up to 80 times a second, and their hearts can beat up to 1200 times a minute!

Other ID: mostly rufous tail. *Male:* orange brown back, tail and flanks; some adult males have green backs. *Female:* red-spotted throat.
Size: L 8–9 cm; W 11.5 cm.
Voice: call is a low *chewp chewp;* also utters a rapid and exuberant confrontation call, *ZEE-chuppity-chup!*
Status: *Coast:* common migrant and breeder. *Interior:* common migrant and breeder south of Prince George; uncommon farther north; rare in the Peace River region.
Habitat: edges of coniferous and deciduous forests, burned sites, brushy slopes, alpine meadows and areas with abundant flowers, including gardens.

Similar Birds

Calliope Hummingbird

Look For

In spring, male Rufous Hummingbirds arrive first, when the early-flowering currants and salmonberry shrubs begin to bloom.

long thin, black bill

green crown

green back

iridescent
orange red
throat

♀

rufous sides
and flanks

white
underparts

white breast
and belly

♂

Nesting: in a tree or shrub; tiny cup nest of plant
down, bark fragments and spider webs is covered
with lichens; white eggs are 13 x 9 mm; female
incubates 2 eggs for 15–17 days; young fledge at
21 days.

Did You Know?

Weighing about as much as a nickel, hummingbirds are
capable of flying at speeds up to 100 km/h.

Belted Kingfisher
Ceryle alcyon

Perched on a bare branch over a productive fish pool, the Belted Kingfisher utters a scratchy, rattling call. Then, with little regard for its scruffy hairdo, the "king of the fishes" plunges headfirst into the water and snags a fish, tadpole or a frog. Back on land, the kingfisher flips its prey into the air and swallows it headfirst. • Kingfisher pairs nest in sandy banks, taking turns digging a tunnel with their sturdy bills and claws. Nest burrows may measure up to 2 metres long and are often found near water.

Other ID: bluish upperparts; white underwings.
Size: *L* 28–36 cm; *W* 51 cm.
Voice: fast, repetitive, cackling rattle, like a teacup shaking on a saucer.
Status: *Coast:* uncommon to common local year-round resident. *Interior:* uncommon local resident year-round in the south-central region; local migrant and breeder elsewhere.
Habitat: rivers, large streams, lakes, marshes and beaver ponds, especially near exposed soil banks, gravel pits or bluffs.

Similar Birds

Blue Jay

Look For

With an extra red band across her belly, the female kingfisher is more colourful than her mate.

shaggy crest

bluish
upperparts

white
"collar"

long,
straight bill

♀

♂

blue grey
breast band

rust-coloured "belt"
on female (may be
incomplete)

no "belt"

Nesting: in a cavity at the end of an earth burrow; glossy white eggs are 34 x 27 mm; pair incubates 6–7 eggs for 22–24 days; both adults feed the young.

Did You Know?

In Greek mythology, Alcyon, the daughter of the wind god, grieved so deeply for her drowned husband that the gods transformed them both into kingfishers.

Downy Woodpecker

Picoides pubescens

A pair of Downy Woodpeckers at your backyard bird feeder will brighten a frosty winter day. These approachable little birds are more tolerant of human activities than most other species, and they visit feeders more often than the larger, more aggressive Hairy Woodpeckers. • Like other woodpeckers, the Downy has evolved special features to help cushion the shock of repeated hammering, including a strong bill and neck muscles, a flexible, reinforced skull and a brain that is tightly packed in its protective cranium.

Other ID: mostly black tail; black-spotted, white outer tail feathers.
Size: *L* 15–18 cm; *W* 30 cm.
Voice: long, unbroken trill; calls are a sharp *pik* or *ki-ki-ki* or whiny *queek queek*.
Status: *Coast:* uncommon resident in the south, including Vancouver I. *Interior:* uncommon resident in the south, including the southern Peace River region.
Habitat: any wooded environment, especially deciduous and mixed forests and areas with tall, deciduous shrubs.

Similar Birds

Hairy
Woodpecker

Red-naped Sapsucker

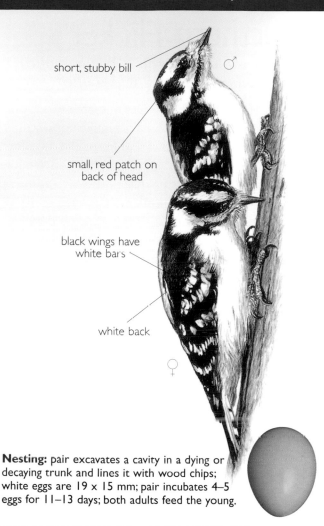

short, stubby bill

♂

small, red patch on
back of head

black wings have
white bars

white back

♀

Nesting: pair excavates a cavity in a dying or
decaying trunk and lines it with wood chips;
white eggs are 19 x 15 mm; pair incubates 4–5
eggs for 11–13 days; both adults feed the young.

Did You Know?

Woodpeckers have feath-
ered nostrils, which filter
out the sawdust produced
when hammering tree
trunks.

Look For

The Downy Woodpecker
uses its small bill to probe
tiny crevices for invertebrates
and wood-boring grubs.

Northern Flicker

Colaptes auratus auratus ("Yellow-shafted")
Colaptes auratus cafer ("Red-shafted")

Instead of boring holes in trees in search of a meal, the Northern Flicker, with its robinlike hops, scours farmlands, grassy meadows and forest clearings for invertebrates, particularly ants. • Flickers often bathe in dusty depressions using dust particles to absorb oils and bacteria. To clean themselves even more thoroughly, flickers squash ants and preen themselves with the remains. Ants contain formic acid, which kills small parasites found on the skin and feathers of this bird. • The "Yellow-shafted" form is found in the north and northeast; the "Red-shafted" is found in the south.

Other ID: white rump; long bill; brown crown; grey face; spotted buff underparts.
Size: *L* 32–33 cm; *W* 51 cm.
Voice: loud, laughing, rapid *kick-kick-kick-kick-kick-kick;* *woika-woika-woika* issued during courtship.
Status: *Coast:* common year-round resident. *Interior:* common year-round resident south of Shuswap L.; common breeder farther north.
Habitat: open deciduous, mixed and coniferous woodlands and forest edges, fields, meadows and farmlands.

Similar Birds

Yellow-bellied
Sapsucker

Red-naped Sapsucker

red "moustache"

black "bib"

♂

no "moustache"

♀

barred, brown back and wings

"Red-shafted Flicker"

Nesting: pair excavates a cavity in a dying or decaying trunk and lines it with wood chips; may also use a nest box; white eggs are 28 x 22 mm; pair incubates 5–8 eggs for 11–16 days.

Did You Know?

Many woodpeckers have zygodactyl feet—two toes face forward and two backward—facilitating vertical movement up and down tree trunks.

Look For

Woodpeckers use their stiff tail feathers to prop up their bodies while they scale trees and excavate cavities.

Pileated Woodpecker
Dryocopus pileatus

The Pileated Woodpecker, with its flaming red crest, chisel-like bill and commanding size, requires at least 40 hectares of mature forest as a breeding territory. Pairs settle in mature forests and may spend up to six weeks excavating a large nest cavity in a dead or decaying tree. • A woodpecker's bill becomes shorter as the bird ages. In his historic painting of the Pileated Woodpecker, John J. Audubon correctly depicted the juvenile birds with slightly longer bills than the adults.

Other ID: white wing linings; white "chin." *Female:* no red "moustache"; red crest.
Size: *L* 41–48 cm; *W* 74 cm.
Voice: loud, fast, rolling *woika-woika-woika-woika;* long series of *kuk* notes; loud, resonant drumming.
Status: *Coast:* uncommon year-round resident on the south inner coast. *Interior:* rare to uncommon year-round resident south of Kamloops and Golden, rare local breeder north to Vanderhoof.
Habitat: mature deciduous, mixed or coniferous forests; also, riparian woodlands or woodlots in suburban and agricultural areas.

Similar Birds

Yellow-bellied
Sapsucker

Red-breasted
Sapsucker

Red-naped Sapsucker

♂

stout,
dark bill

red crest
(extends from bill
to nape)

red "moustache"

yellow eyes

white stripe
extends from bill
to shoulder

♀

adult pair

Nesting: pair excavates a cavity in a dying or decaying trunk and lines it with wood chips; white eggs are 33 × 25 mm; pair incubates 4 eggs for 15–18 days; both adults feed the young.

Did You Know?

Ducks, small falcons, owls and even flying squirrels frequently nest in abandoned Pileated Woodpecker cavities.

Look For

Foraging Pileated Woodpeckers leave elliptical cavities and large holes at the base of trees.

Olive-sided Flycatcher
Contopus cooperi

The Olive-sided Flycatcher's upright, attentive posture contrasts with its comical call: *quick-three-beers! quick-three-beers!* Like a dutiful parent, this flycatcher changes its tune during nesting season to a more conservative, but equally enthusiastic *pip-pip-pip.* • Olive-sided Flycatchers nest high in the forest canopy. Far above the forest floor, they have easy access to an abundance of flying insects, including honeybees and adult wood-boring and bark beetles.

Other ID: white tufts on sides of rump; dark upper mandible; dull yellow orange base to lower mandible; inconspicuous eye ring.

Size: *L* 18–20 cm; *W* 33 cm.

Voice: *Male:* song is a chipper and lively *quick-three-beers!,* with the second note highest in pitch; descending *pip-pip-pip* when excited.

Status: *Coast:* uncommon migrant and breeder in the south. *Interior:* uncommon migrant and breeder.

Habitat: semi-open mixed and coniferous forests near water; prefers burned areas and wetlands.

Similar Birds

Western Wood-Pewee

Eastern Phoebe

Eastern Kingbird

olive grey to
olive brown
upperparts

light throat
and belly

dark, olive
grey "vest"

Nesting: high in a conifer, usually on a branch far
from the trunk; nest of twigs and plant fibres is
bound with spider silk; darkly spotted, white to
pinkish buff eggs are 22 x 16 mm; female incubates 3 eggs for 14–17 days.

Did You Know?

Olive-sided Flycatchers
are fierce nest defenders
and will harass and chase
off squirrels and other
predators.

Look For

A big-headed silhouette on
the tip of a mature conifer or
dead branch may well belong
to this feisty flycatcher.

Northern Shrike
Lanius excubitor

The Northern Shrike is one of the most vicious predatorial songbirds, relying on its sharp, hooked bill to catch and kill small birds and rodents. Its tendency to impale its prey on thorns and barbs for later consumption has earned it the name "Butcher Bird." Its scientific name means "watchful butcher," which appropriately describes the shrike's foraging behaviour. • Northern Shrikes, true to their name, summer only in the far northwest of the province.

Other ID: black "mask" does not extend above hooked bill. *In flight:* white wing patches; white-edged tail.
Size: *L* 25 cm; *W* 37 cm.
Voice: usually silent; occasionally gives a long grating laugh: *raa-raa-raa-raa*.
Status: *Coast:* uncommon migrant and winter visitor in the south; rare in the north. *Interior:* uncommon migrant and winter visitor; breeds only in the extreme northwest.
Habitat: open country, including fields, shrubby areas, forest clearings and roadsides.

Similar Birds

Loggerhead Shrike

Northern Mockingbird

juvenile

hooked bill

black tail and wings

finely barred, pale underparts

white outer tail feathers

Nesting: on the taiga in a spruce, willow or shrub; nest is made of sticks, bark and moss; darkly spotted, greenish white to pale grey eggs are 29 x 19 mm; female incubates 4–7 eggs for 15–17 days.

Did You Know?

Shrikes are the world's only true carnivorous songbirds. Africa and Eurasia boast the greatest diversity of shrike species.

Look For

Northern Shrikes typically perch at the tops of tall trees to survey an area for prey. They have a distinctive, upright silhouette that, with practice, is easy to recognize.

Warbling Vireo
Vireo gilvus

The Warbling Vireo is becoming increasingly common and widespread in British Columbia, but still, you might have to look hard to find one. These smoky coloured birds are difficult to spot because they are slow, deliberate and lack any splashy field marks. • This bird ranks high among our province's songsters. The oscillating, warbled quality of its squeaky song delights all listeners, with some phrases ending on an upbeat as if asking a question. Once the velvety voice of the Warbling Vireo is learned, auditory encounters may offer clues to the whereabouts of this inconspicuous bird.

Other ID: slender body; no wing bars.
Size: *L* 14 cm; *W* 22 cm.
Voice: male's song is *I love you I love you Ma'am!* or *iggly wiggly iggly piggly iggly eeek!;* females occasionally sing from the nest; both male and female give a *sneer* note.
Status: *Coast:* common summer visitor in south, uncommon in north. *Interior:* uncommon in the northwest; common breeder elsewhere.
Habitat: varied riparian woodlands and mixed deciduous-coniferous forests from sea level to 1500 m.

Similar Birds

Red-eyed Vireo   Cassin's Vireo   Hutton's Vireo   Orange-crowned Warbler

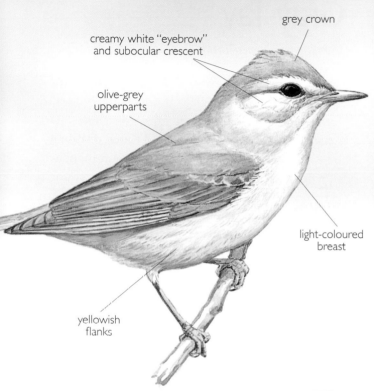

grey crown

creamy white "eyebrow" and subocular crescent

olive-grey upperparts

light-coloured breast

yellowish flanks

Nesting: in a fork in a deciduous tree or shrub; hanging cup nest of grasses, roots, plant down, spider's silk and feathers; white eggs with reddish-brown spots are 19 x 14 mm; pair incubates 4 eggs for 12 days.

Did You Know?

Warbling Vireos breed across North America and have the largest breeding range of all vireos on our continent.

Look For

Warbling Vireos flit among the branches in open, leafy forests or orchards; they tend to avoid mature forests.

Gray Jay

Perisoreus canadensis

The friendly, mischievous Gray Jay sports a dark grey cloak and a long, elegant tail. These bold birds form strong pair bonds, and after an absence, partners will seek each other out and touch or nibble bills. • Gray Jays lay their eggs and begin incubation as early as late February, allowing the young to get a head start on learning to forage and to store food. These birds cache food for the winter, and their specialized salivary glands coat the food with a sticky mucus that helps to preserve it.

Other ID: fluffy, pale grey plumage; dark grey nape and upperparts; white undertail coverts.
Size: *L* 28–33 cm; *W* 45 cm.
Voice: calls include a soft, whistled *quee-oo,* a chuckled *cla-cla-cla* and a *churr;* also imitates other birds.
Status: *Coast:* uncommon resident on Vancouver I, Lower Mainland and adjacent mountains. *Interior:* uncommon to locally common resident.
Habitat: dense and open coniferous and mixed forests, bogs and fens; picnic sites and campgrounds.

Similar Birds

Northern Shrike (p. 112)

Loggerhead Shrike

Clark's Nutcracker

white "cheek"

dark bill

light grey
breast and belly

long tail

Nesting: in a conifer; insulated nest is made of
plant fibres, roots, mosses, twigs, feathers and fur;
speckled, pale grey to greenish eggs are 29 x 21 mm;
female incubates 3–4 eggs for 17–22 days.

Did You Know?

The Gray's nickname
"Whiskey Jack" comes
from its Algonquin name,
wis-kat-jon; other names
include "Canada Jay" and
"Camp Robber."

Look For

In flight, the Gray Jay has a
distinctive bounce with alter-
nating fast flaps and short
glides, usually performed
close to the ground.

Steller's Jay
Cyanocitta stelleri

The stunning Steller's Jay is a resident jewel in our southern and coastal forests. Generally noisy and pugnacious, this bird suddenly becomes silent and cleverly elusive when nesting. • Bold Steller's Jays will not hesitate to steal food scraps from inattentive picnickers and scatter smaller birds at feeders. Their ability to adapt and learn suggests that corvids are very intelligent birds. • George Wilhelm Steller, the first European naturalist to visit Alaska, was convinced he had arrived in North America when he mistook the Steller's Jay for the similar Blue Jay he had seen in paintings.

Other ID: black head, nape and back. *In flight:* grayish underwings with blue linings; round-tipped blue tails; makes short glides and upward lift.

Size: *L* 22 cm; *W* 48 cm.

Voice: harsh, far-carrying *shack-shack-shack;* a grating *kresh, kresh.*

Status: *Coast:* uncommon breeding resident. *Interior:* uncommon resident from southern Peace River and Prince George southward, rare elsewhere.

Habitat: coniferous forests and pine–oak woodlands to 2600 m, occasionally higher; townsites and exotic tree plantations.

Similar Birds

Blue Jay

Gray Jay (p. 116)

bluish forehead streaks

prominent, shaggy crest

glossy, deep velvet blue plumage

wings and tail are barred

Nesting: in the fork of a conifer; bulky stick and twig nest is lined with mud, grass and conifer needles; brown-marked, pale greenish blue eggs are 31 x 22 mm; female incubates 4 eggs for 16 days.

Did You Know?

Residents of British Columbia selected the Steller's Jay as their provincial bird in 1987.

Look For

Steller's Jays occur west of and in the Rocky Mountains; the similar looking Blue Jay lives to the east of the Rockies.

American Crow
Corvus brachyrhynchos

The noise that emanates from this treetop squawker seems not to be representative of its intelligence. These wary, clever birds are impressive mimics, able to whine like a dog and laugh or cry like a human. • Crows are family-oriented, and the young from the previous year help their parents to raise the next year's nestlings. • American Crows are ecological generalists, able to adapt to a variety of habitats. The Northwestern Crow is the equivalent to the American Crow, but is only found on the west coast, whereas, the American is found throughout the southern two-thirds of British Columbia.

Other ID: slim, sleek head and throat.
Size: *L* 43–53 cm; *W* 94 cm.
Voice: distinctive, far-carrying, repetitive *caw-caw-caw*.
Status: *Coast:* absent. *Interior:* common migrant and summer visitant south of Peace River and Smithers; uncommon, local resident from the Cariboo south.
Habitat: urban areas, agricultural fields and other open areas with scattered woodlands, marshes, lakes and rivers in densely forested areas.

Similar Birds

Common Raven (p. 122)

Black-billed Magpie

Northwestern Crow

square-shaped tail

black bill

glossy, purple
black plumage

black legs

Nesting: in a coniferous or deciduous tree or on a utility pole; large stick-and-branch nest is lined with fur and soft plant materials; darkly blotched, grey green to blue green eggs are 41 x 29 mm; female incubates 4–6 eggs for about 18 days.

Did You Know?

American Crows group together in fall in large flocks known as "murders."

Look For

Crows and ravens are similar in appearance. To distinguish them, look for the crow's squared tail and slim beak and the raven's wedge-shaped tail and heavier bill.

Common Raven

Corvus corax

The Common Raven soars with a wingspan comparable to that of hawk's, travelling along coastlines, over arid deserts, along mountain ridges and even on the arctic tundra. Few birds occupy such a large natural range. • Like crows, ravens are intelligent members of the corvid family and maintain loyal, lifelong pair bonds. When working as a pair to confiscate a meal, one raven may act as the decoy while the other steals the food. Their courtship behaviour sends them tumbling through space together, talons locked.

Other ID: *In flight:* soars and performs acrobatics.
Size: *L* 61 cm; *W* 1.3 m.
Voice: deep, guttural, far-carrying, repetitive *craww-craww* or *quork quork* among other vocalizations.
Status: *Coast:* uncommon resident.
Interior: uncommon resident; locally abundant at landfills.
Habitat: coniferous and mixed forests, alpine, mountains and marshes; townsites and landfills.

Similar Birds

American Crow (p. 120)

Look For

The Common Raven is glorified in many cultures, especially among native cultures, as a magical being, and exhibits some behaviours that are uncannily human.

rounded wings

black upperparts

heavy, black bill

shaggy throat

all-black plumage

wedge-shaped tail

Nesting: on a rock ledge, bluff, bridge or in a tall coniferous tree; large stick-and-branch nest is lined with fur and soft plant materials; variably marked, greenish eggs are 50 x 33 mm; female incubates 4–6 eggs for 18–21 days.

Did You Know?

Ravens survive the harsher environments of the north in B.C. with some help from the predators of the food chain. For example, the Common Raven feeds on the carrion of a hunted elk left by a wolf. This bird can live for up to 40 years!

Horned Lark
Eremophila alpestris

An impressive, high-speed, plummeting courtship dive would blow anybody's hair back, or in the case of the Horned Lark, its two unique, black horns. Long before the snow is gone, this bird's tinkling song will be one of the first you hear to introduce spring. • Horned Larks are often abundant at roadsides, searching for seeds, but an approaching vehicle usually sends them flying into an adjacent field, making it difficult to identify them. When these birds visit in winter, you can spot them in farmers' fields or catch them at the beach visiting with Snow Buntings and Lapland Longspurs.

Other ID: *Female:* duller plumage.
Size: *L* 18 cm; *W* 30 cm.
Voice: call is a tinkling *tsee-titi* or *zoot;* flight song is a long series of tinkling, twittered whistles.
Status: *Coast:* rare year-round resident; uncommon migrant; extirpated breeder. *Interior:* common to abundant migrant and locally common breeder; less common in Peace River region.
Habitat: *Breeding:* open areas, including pastures, rangeland, airfields and alpine tundra. *In migration* and *winter:* croplands, roadside ditches and fields.

Similar Birds

Snow Bunting

Lapland Longspur

American Pipit

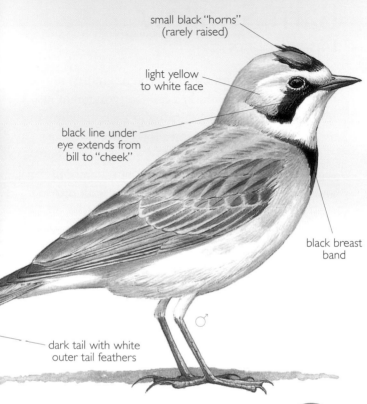

small black "horns"
(rarely raised)

light yellow
to white face

black line under
eye extends from
bill to "cheek"

black breast
band

♂

dark tail with white
outer tail feathers

Nesting: on the ground; in a shallow scrape lined with grasses, plant fibres and roots; brown-blotched, grey to greenish white eggs are 23 x 16 mm; female incubates 3–4 eggs for 10–12 days.

Did You Know?

One way to distinguish a sparrow from a Horned Lark is by their method of travel: Horned Larks walk and sparrows hop.

Look For

The Horned Lark's dark tail contrasts with its light brown body and belly and is a great field mark to identify these birds in their open-country habitat.

Barn Swallow
Hirundo rustica

In an encounter with this bird, you might first notice its distinctive, deeply forked tail—or you might just find yourself repeatedly ducking to avoid the dives of a protective parent. Barn Swallows once nested on cliffs, but they are now found more frequently nesting on human-made structures. Barns, boathouses and areas under bridges and house eaves all provide shelter from predators and inclement weather. The messy, growing young and aggressive parents unfortunately often bring people to remove nests just as nesting season is beginning, but this bird's close association with humans allows us to observe the normally secretive reproductive cycle of birds.

Other ID: blue black upperparts; long, pointed wings.
Size: *L* 18 cm; *W* 38 cm.
Voice: continuous, twittering chatter: *zip-zip-zip* or *kvick-kvick*.
Status: *Coast:* common to locally abundant migrant and common breeder. *Interior:* common to locally abundant migrant and common breeder in the south; less common farther north.
Habitat: open rural and urban areas where bridges, culverts and buildings are found near water.

Similar Birds

Cliff Swallow

Purple Martin

Tree Swallow

rufous throat
and forehead

rust- to buff-coloured
underparts

long, deeply
forked tail

Nesting: singly or in small, loose colonies; on a human-made structure under an overhang; half or full cup nest is made of mud, grass and straw; brown-spotted, white eggs are 20 x 14 mm; pair incubates 4–7 eggs for 13–17 days.

Did You Know?

The Barn Swallow is a natural pest controller, feeding on insects that are often harmful to crops and livestock.

Look For

Barn Swallows roll mud into small balls and build their nests one mouthful of mud at a time.

Black-capped Chickadee
Poecile atricapillus

Black-capped Chickadees are an incredibly sociable bird. In winter, they join the company of kinglets, nuthatches, creepers and small woodpeckers to feed; in spring and fall, they migrate in mixed flocks of vireos and warblers. • While observing their antics at feeders, you may be able to entice a Black-capped Chickadee to the palm of your hand with the help of a sunflower seed. • On cold nights, chickadees enter into a hypothermic state, lowering their body temperature and heartbeat considerably so as to conserve energy.

Other ID: black "bib"; dark legs.
Size: *L* 13–15 cm; *W* 20 cm.
Voice: call is a chipper, whistled *chick-a-dee-dee-dee;* song is a slow, whistled *swee-tee* or *fee-bee.*
Status: *Coast:* common breeding year-round resident in Lower Mainland. *Interior:* common breeding resident in the south; uncommon breeding resident in the north.
Habitat: deciduous and mixed forests, riparian woodlands, wooded urban parks; backyard feeders.

Similar Birds

Mountain Chickadee

Boreal Chickadee

Blackpoll Warbler

black "cap"

white "cheek"

grey back
and wings

white edging on
wing feathers

white
underparts

Nesting: pair excavates a cavity in a rotting tree or stump; cavity is lined with fur, feathers, moss, grass and cocoons; occasionally uses a birdhouse; finely speckled, white eggs are 15 x 12 mm; female incubates 6–8 eggs for 12–13 days.

Did You Know?

Black-capped Chickadees are thought to possess amazing memories. They can relocate seed caches up to a month after they are hidden!

Look For

The Black-capped Chickadee sometimes feeds while hanging upside down, giving it the chance to grab a meal another bird may not be able to reach.

Chestnut-backed Chickadee

Poecile rufescens

A Chestnut-backed Chickadee could fit in the palm of your hand, but these energetic little birds would hardly sit still long enough. They prefer to flit through the forest and scour for insects or descend on bird feeders in merry mobs. To view these friendly birds up close, mount a platform feeder on your window ledge. • On chilly winter days, chickadees must work hard to survive. They sometimes depend on food stores stashed during the summer, and they stay warm by snuggling together in crevices or woodpecker cavities.

Other ID: pale underparts; dark greyish wings and tail.
Size: *L* 14 cm; *W* 19 cm.
Voice: gives higher, buzzier call notes than other chickadees, song is a *chip* series.
Status: *Coast:* common breeding resident. *Interior:* uncommon breeding resident in the south.
Habitat: coniferous, hardwood and mixed forests of any kind; uses various native and exotic trees in residential areas; backyard feeders.

Similar Birds

Mountain Chickadee

Black-capped Chickadee (p. 128)

dark brown "cap"

white "cheek"

rich chestnut-brown back and sides

black "bib"

Nesting: excavates a cavity in a rotting tree-trunk or uses a natural cavity or abandoned woodpecker nest; rufous-marked, white eggs are 15 x 12 mm; pair incubates 6–7 eggs for up to 15 days.

Did You Know?

Bumblebees intent on establishing a new hive have been known to invade a chickadee cavity, chasing the small bird from its nesting space.

Look For

In winter, Chestnut-backed Chickadees join groups of kinglets, Red-breasted Nuthatches and Brown Creepers.

Red-breasted Nuthatch

Sitta canadensis

The Red-breasted Nuthatch may look like a wood-pecker, but its view of the world could be considered somewhat dizzying. This interesting bird, with its distinctive black eye line and red breast, moves down tree trunks headfirst, cleaning up the seeds, insects and fruits that woodpeckers may have overlooked. • The odd name "nuthatch" comes from this bird's habit of wedging large seeds into crevices, then using its bill to hammer them open. • Its species name, *canadensis,* means "of Canada."

Other ID: white "cheek"; black "cap"; straight bill; short tail. *Male:* deeper rust on breast.
Size: *L* 11 cm; *W* 21 cm.
Voice: call is a slow, repeated, nasal *yank yank yank;* also a short *tsip.*
Status: *Coast:* uncommon resident in the south; rare breeding resident in the north. *Interior:* common resident in the south; uncommon migrant and breeder northward.
Habitat: *Breeding:* mixed coniferous and deciduous forests. *In migration* and *winter:* mixed woodlands, especially those near bird feeders.

Similar Birds

White-breasted
Nuthatch

Brown Creeper (p. 134)

Pygmy Nuthatch

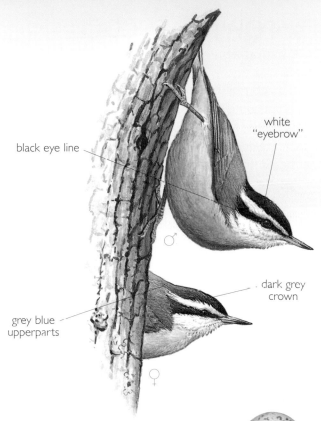

black eye line

white "eyebrow"

♂

dark grey crown

grey blue upperparts

♀

Nesting: excavates a cavity or uses an abandoned woodpecker nest; nest is made of bark shreds, grass and fur with sap spread at entrance; brown-spotted, white eggs are 15 × 12 mm; female incubates 5–6 eggs for about 12 days.

Did You Know?

These birds smear their nest entrance with sap to keep ants and other insects away; these creatures can transmit fungal infections or parasitize nestlings.

Look For

The Red-breasted Nuthatch visits feeders, but you may only catch a glimpse of its red belly when it grabs a sunflower seed and darts away to eat it in private.

Brown Creeper
Certhia americana

The cryptic Brown Creeper is never easy to find, often going unnoticed until a flake of bark suddenly takes the shape of a bird. A frightened creeper will freeze and flatten itself against a tree trunk, becoming nearly invisible. • The Brown Creeper uses its long, stiff tail feathers to prop itself up while climbing vertical tree trunks. When it reaches the upper branches, it floats down to the base of a neighbouring tree to begin another foraging ascent.

Other ID: rusty rump.
Size: *L* 13 cm; *W* 19 cm.
Voice: song is a faint, high-pitched *trees-trees-trees see the trees;* call is a high *tseee.*
Status: *Coast:* uncommon year-round.
Interior: uncommon year-round in the south; locally rare migrant and summer visitor in the north.
Habitat: old-growth and mature deciduous, coniferous forests, especially with large snags.

Similar Birds

Red-breasted Nuthatch (p. 132)

Pygmy Nuthatch

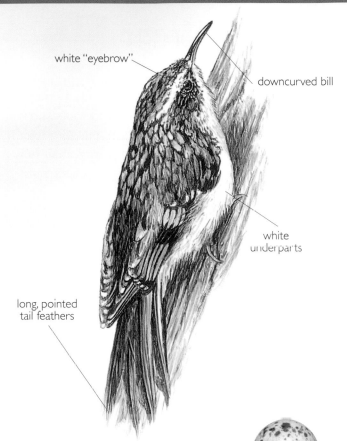

white "eyebrow"

downcurved bill

white underparts

long, pointed tail feathers

Nesting: under loose bark; nest of grasses and conifer needles is woven together with spider silk; brown-spotted, whitish eggs are 15 x 12 mm; female incubates 5–6 eggs for 14–17 days.

Did You Know?

There are many species of creepers in Europe and Asia, but the Brown Creeper is the only member of its family found in North America.

Look For

The Brown Creeper feeds by slowly spiraling up a tree trunk, searching for hidden invertebrates.

Winter Wren
Troglodytes troglodytes

The upraised, mottled brown tail of the Winter Wren matches the gnarled, upturned roots and decomposing tree trunks it calls home. Although it blends well with its habitat, you may wonder how something so small could have such vocal magnitude—it boldly lays claim to its territory with its call and distinctive, melodious song. • Though the male Winter Wren contributes to raising the family, defending the nest and finding food for the nestlings, he sleeps elsewhere at night, usually in an unfinished nest.

Other ID: dark brown upperparts; lighter brown underparts.
Size: *L* 10 cm; *W* 14 cm.
Voice: *Male:* song is a warbled, tinkling series of quick trills and twitters, up to 10 seconds long; call is a sharp *chip-chip*.
Status: *Coast:* common year-round. *Interior:* rare resident in south, uncommon migrant and summer visitor in central, and rare migrant in north.
Habitat: mature fir, hemlock and cedar forests, often near water; moist boreal forests; shrubby areas in migration.

Similar Birds

House Wren

Marsh Wren

very short, stubby, upraised tail

fine, pale buff "eyebrow"

prominent, dark barring on flanks

Nesting: in a natural cavity, under bark or under upturned tree roots; nest is made of twigs, moss, grass and fur; male builds up to 4 "dummy" nests; white eggs with reddish-brown dots are 18 x 13 mm; female incubates 5–7 eggs for 14–16 days.

Did You Know?

The Winter Wren, often called the "Jenny Wren," can sustain its song for 10 seconds using up to 113 tones.

Look For

This bird has a habit of bobbing its entire body up and down as if it were doing push-ups.

Golden-crowned Kinglet
Regulus satrapa

You might just barely detect this kinglet's call above a slight woodland breeze. The dainty Golden-crowned Kinglet is not much bigger than a hummingbird and when it gleans for insects, berries and sap in the forest canopy, it is prone to being attacked by predators such as the Sharp-shinned Hawk. • "Pishing" and squeaking sounds might lure these songbirds into an observable range, and behavioural traits, such as its perpetual motion and chronic wing flicking, can help identify Golden-crowns from a distance.

Other ID: light underparts.
Size: *L* 10 cm; *W* 18 cm.
Voice: song is a faint, high-pitched, accelerating *tsee-tsee-tsee-tsee, why do you shilly-shally?*; call is a very high-pitched *tsee tsee tsee*.
Status: *Coast:* uncommon year-round. *Interior:* uncommon year-round in the south; uncommon migrant and summer visitor elsewhere.
Habitat: *Breeding:* dense spruce, western hemlock, Douglas-fir and alpine forests. *In migration* and *winter:* deciduous and mixed forests and woodlands.

Similar Birds

Ruby-crowned Kinglet

Black-capped Chickadee (p. 128)

Boreal Chickadee

yellow crown with
black border

2 white wing bars

reddish orange
crown

♂

♀

white
"eyebrow"

Nesting: usually in a spruce or other conifer; hanging nest is made of mosses, lichens, twigs and leaves; pale buff eggs spotted with grey and brown are 13 x 10 mm; female incubates 8–9 eggs for 14–15 days.

Did You Know?

The Golden-crowned Kinglet's scientific name, *Regulus,* is from the Latin word for "king," a fitting name for a bird that wears a golden crown!

Look For

Golden-crowns are often joined by migrating and foraging flocks of chickadees, Red-breasted Nuthatches and Brown Creepers in the tops of trees throughout B.C.

Mountain Bluebird
Sialia currucoides

Vibrant Mountain Bluebirds look like a piece of sky come to life. They perch on wire fences and fence posts, alighting to snatch up insects on the ground. • Natural nest sites, such as woodpecker cavities, are in high demand in breeding season. Habitat loss and increased competition with aggressive European Starlings have forced many bluebirds to nest in artificial nest boxes. A growing number of volunteer-monitored "bluebird trails" encourage bluebirds to breed in our region's rural areas.

Other ID: upperparts are darker than the underparts; grey underparts.
Size: *L* 18 cm; *W* 36 cm.
Voice: call is a low *turr turr;* male's song is a short warble of churs.
Status: *Coast:* uncommon migrant and rare breeder in the Lower Mainland; rare elsewhere. *Interior:* common migrant and breeder in the south and southern Peace River; rare in the north.
Habitat: *Breeding:* open parkland, rangeland and subalpine from sea level to 2700 m. *In migration:* alpine grasslands, forest edges, clearcuts and agricultural fields.

Similar Birds

Western Bluebird

Townsend's Solitaire

Lazuli Bunting

blue grey back and head

black eyes and bill

♀

♂

sky blue body

black legs

Nesting: in an abandoned woodpecker cavity, natural cavity or nest box; cavity is lined with plant stems, grasses, small twigs and feathers; female incubates 5–6 pale blue eggs for 13 days.

Did You Know?

Mountain Bluebirds often raise two broods per year. Fledglings of the first nesting may help to gather food for the second.

Look For

Recently burned and logged areas attract bluebirds, which nest in abandoned woodpecker cavities in standing snags.

Swainson's Thrush
Catharus ustulatus

This bird, once known as the "Olive-backed Thrush," usually sings the last song heard at nightfall. The Swainson's Thrush shares the speckled breast of a few other B.C. thrushes. It forages mainly on the ground for insects and other invertebrates, but you may also catch this bird hover-gleaning from the airy heights of trees like a warbler or vireo does. • The Swainson's is a wary bird and often gives its sharp warning call from a distance, not giving itself much chance to be seen.

Other ID: buff wash on "cheek" and upper breast.
Size: *L* 18 cm; *W* 29 cm.
Voice: song is a slow, rolling, rising spiral: *Oh, Aurelia will-ya, will-ya will-yeee;* call is a sharp *wick* or *prit.*
Status: *Coast:* common migrant and breeder. *Interior:* common migrant and breeder in the south; less common in the north.
Habitat: edges and openings of young to mature coniferous and mixed forests; prefers areas with dense undergrowth of tall shrubs.

Similar Birds

Gray-cheeked Thrush

Hermit Thrush

Veery

buff eye ring

streaks of spots
on throat and
breast

brownish
grey flanks

Nesting: usually in a shrub or small tree; cup
nest is made of grasses, mosses, roots and leaves,
lined with with fur; brown spotted, pale blue eggs
are 22 x 17 mm; female incubates 3–4 eggs for
12–14 days.

Did You Know?

Rather than descending
like other *Catharus* species,
such as the Hermit Thrush,
the song of the Swainson's
Thrush has rapid, flutelike
notes that spiral upward.

Look For

In breeding season, you can
frequently spot this bird feeding at the edge of country
roads as the sunlight fades.

American Robin
Turdus migratorius

Come March, the familiar song of the American Robin may wake you early if you are a light sleeper. This abundant bird adapts easily to urban areas and often works from dawn until after dusk when there is a nest to be built or hungry, young mouths to feed. • The robin's bright red belly contrasted with its dark head and wings make the robin easy to identify even for a nonbirder. • In fall, these birds gather in berry trees and shrubs to fill energy stores before continuing their journey southward.

Other ID: black-tipped, yellow bill.
Size: *L* 25 cm; *W* 43 cm.
Voice: song is an even warble: *cheerily cheer-up cheerio;* call is a rapid *tut-tut-tut.*
Status: *Coast:* common resident in the south; common migrant and breeder in the north. *Interior:* abundant migrant, common breeder, uncommon in winter in the south; common migrant and breeder in the north.
Habitat: urban and residential lawns, gardens and parks, pastures, mixed young forests, wetlands and river and lake shorelines.

Similar Birds

Varied Thrush (p. 146)

Look For

In B.C., summer birds travel south in fall and some are replaced by northern breeders, giving the impression of year-round presence.

black head

incomplete
white eye ring

light red
orange breast

♂   ♀

white undertail
coverts

deep brick red
breast

Nesting: in a coniferous or deciduous tree or shrub or on a building beam; cup nest is built of grasses, mosses, plant stems and mud; light blue eggs are 28 x 20 mm; female incubates 4 eggs for 11–16 days; raises up to 3 broods per year.

Did You Know?

A hunting robin with its head tilted to the side isn't listening for prey, but rather is looking for movements in the soil, waiting for its next meal to come to the surface.

Varied Thrush
Ixoreus naevius

The haunting courtship song of the Varied Thrush is unlike any other. The melodic tones of its long, drawn-out hum penetrate well through the dense vegetation and drifting mist enshrouding this bird's forest habitat. • Early spring usually proves to be the harshest time of year because food supplies and fat reserves are at a minimum. During cold autumn weather, many Varied Thrushes, along with other songbirds, migrate to lowland valleys and towns where food is more readily available.

Other ID: *Female:* similar to male, but duller colouring; brown upperparts; fainter breast band.
Size: *L* 24 cm; *W* 34–41 cm.
Voice: male's song is a series of sustained single notes delivered at different pitches, with a pause between each note; call is a rich *chuck*.
Status: *Coast:* year-round resident, less common in summer at low elevations. *Interior:* common summer visitor and breeder; rare to uncommon in winter.
Habitat: cool, humid coniferous forests with a dense understorey; mixed, dense riparian woodlands in canyons, ravines and gullies; at feeders in winter.

Similar Birds

American Robin (p. 144)

Look For

Look low for Varied Thurshes—these beautiful birds spend a lot of time on the ground, searching through the damp forest litter for insects, seeds and berries.

orange "eyebrow"

2 orange
wing bars

♀

orange
throat
and belly

deep blue black
upperparts

black
breast band

♂

Nesting: often against the trunk of a conifer;
bulky cup nest is made of twigs, leaves, mosses and
grass; light blue, unmarked eggs are 30 x 21 mm;
female incubates 3–4 eggs for 14 days.

Did You Know?

If threatened, the Varied Thrush will crouch low with its neck
extended and feathers sleek, then lift its tail and spread its
wings forward to intimidate an intruder.

European Starling

Sturnus vulgaris

The European Starling did not hesitate to make itself known across North America after being released in New York's Central Park in 1890 and 1891. These highly adaptable birds not only took over the nesting sites of native cavity nesters, such as Tree Swallows and Mountain Bluebirds, but they learned to mimic the sounds of Killdeers, Red-tailed Hawks, Soras and Meadowlarks. European Starlings have even out-competed the also introduced Crested Myna from Southeast Asia. • Look for massive evening roosts of European Starlings under bridges, on buildings or in boulevard trees.

Other ID: dark eyes; short, squared tail.
Size: *L* 22 cm; *W* 40 cm.
Voice: variety of whistles, squeaks, and gurgles; imitates other birds.
Status: *Coast:* abundant resident in the south; uncommon resident in the north. *Interior:* common resident in the south, uncommon migrant and breeder in the north.
Habitat: agricultural areas, townsites, woodland edges, landfills and roadsides.

Similar Birds

Rusty Blackbird

Brown-headed Cowbird (p. 174)

Brewer's Blackbird

iridescent, purple
black head and neck

glossy, green back
with buffy spots

yellow bill

greenish black
underparts

breeding

Nesting: in an abandoned woodpecker cavity,
natural cavity or nest box; nest is made of grass,
twigs and straw; bluish to greenish white eggs
are 30 x 21 mm; female incubates 4–6 eggs for
12–14 days.

Did You Know?

This bird was brought to
New York as part of the
local Shakespeare society's
plan to introduce all the
birds mentioned in their
favourite author's writings.

Look For

The European Starling has
the characteristics of a blackbird. Look for the starling's
comparably shorter tail and
bright yellow bill to help you
accurately identify it.

Cedar Waxwing
Bombycilla cedrorum

With its black "mask" and slick hairdo, the Cedar Waxwing has a heroic look. The splendid personality of this bird is reflected in its amusing antics after it gorges on fermented berries, or in the performance of its gentle courtship dance. To court a mate, the gentlemanly male hops toward a female and offers her a berry. The female accepts the berry and hops away, then stops and hops back toward the male to offer him the berry in return.

Other ID: brown upperparts; grey rump; yellow terminal tail band.
Size: *L* 18 cm; *W* 30 cm.
Voice: faint, high-pitched, trilled whistle: *tseee-tseee-tseee.*
Status: *Coast:* common summer visitor and breeder in the south; uncommon in the north. *Interior:* common summer visitor and breeder in the south; uncommon in southern Peace River; rare elsewhere.
Habitat: shrubby forest edges, second-growth, riparian and open woodlands and wooded residential parks and gardens.

Similar Birds

Bohemian Waxwing

Look For

The Bohemian Waxwing, a cousin of the Cedar Waxwing, nests in the north, and roving bands sometimes make an appearance in winter to feed on mountain ash berries.

cinnamon crest

black "mask"

small red "drops" on wings

yellow wash on belly

white undertail coverts

Nesting: in a young coniferous or deciduous tree or shrub; cup nest is made of twigs, mosses and lichens; darkly spotted, bluish to grey eggs are 22 x 16 mm; female incubates 3–5 eggs for 12–16 days.

Did You Know?

It is suspected by many that the yellow tail band and "waxy" red wing tips of the Cedar Waxwing get their colour from pigments in the berries that these birds eat.

Yellow Warbler
Dendroica petechia

The Yellow Warbler is often parasitized by the Brown-headed Cowbird and can recognize cowbird eggs, but rather than tossing them out, will build another nest overtop the old eggs or abandon the nest completely. Occasionally, cowbirds strike repeatedly—a stack of five warbler nests was once found! • The Yellow Warbler is often mistakenly thought to be a "Wild Canary." It flits from branch to branch in search of juicy caterpillars, aphids and beetles.

Other ID: yellowish legs; bright yellow highlights on dark yellow olive tail and wings.
Size: *L* 13 cm; *W* 20 cm.
Voice: song is a fast, frequently repeated *sweet-sweet-sweet summer sweet.*
Status: *Coast:* common migrant and breeder on inner south coast; uncommon to rare elsewhere. *Interior:* uncommon to common migrant and breeder.
Habitat: moist, open woodlands with dense, low scrub; shrubby meadows, willow tangles, shrubby fencerows and riparian swamps; usually near water.

Similar Birds

Orange-crowned Warbler

American Goldfinch (p. 180)

Common Yellowthroat (p. 156)

Wilson's Warbler

black bill
and eyes

bright yellow
body

faint, red
breast streaks

red breast
streaks

♀

♂

breeding

Nesting: in a deciduous tree or shrub; female
builds a cup nest of grass, weeds and shredded
bark; darkly speckled, greenish white eggs are
17 x 13 mm; female incubates eggs for 11–12 days.

Did You Know?

Found throughout North
America and on Central
and South American
Islands, the Yellow Warbler
has an amazing geographi-
cal range for a small bird.

Look For

In fall migration, when male
Yellow Warblers no longer
wear their breeding plumage,
look for the flashes of yellow
on the sides of their tails to
distinguish them.

Yellow-rumped Warbler

Dendroica coronata auduboni ("Audubon's")
Dendroica coronata coronate ("Myrtle")

In British Columbia, the Yellow-rumped Warbler comes in two forms: the common, yellow-throated "Audubon's Warbler" of the south and the white-throated "Myrtle Warbler" of the north. They were once considered separate species, but because of overlapping ranges, ability to interbreed and close genetic similarities, they are now considered a single species.

Other ID: *"Audubon's Warbler"*: yellow crown, chin, throat, side patches and rump; white belly, undertail coverts and undertail patch. *Breeding male:* blue grey to blackish head, breast, sides and back. *Breeding female:* fainter yellow patches.

Size: L 14 cm; W 22 cm.

Voice: male's song is a rising or falling warble; call is a sharp *chip* or *chet*.

Status: *Coast:* common migrant and uncommon breeder in the south; less common on north mainland; rare migrant on Queen Charlotte Is. *Interior:* abundant migrant and common breeder.

Habitat: *Breeding:* mixed coniferous forests and riparian woodlands. *In migration:* mixed coniferous and deciduous forests, riparian shrublands, transmission corridors and lakeshores.

Similar Birds

Townsend's Warbler

Palm Warbler

Magnolia Warbler

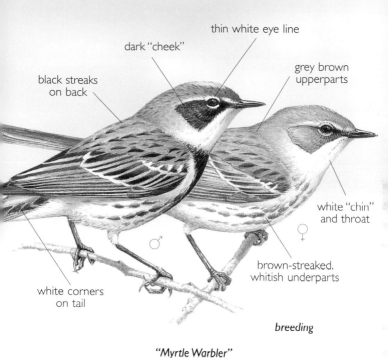

thin white eye line

dark "cheek"

grey brown
upperparts

black streaks
on back

white "chin"
and throat

♂

♀

brown-streaked,
whitish underparts

white corners
on tail

breeding

"Myrtle Warbler"

Nesting: in a crotch or on a horizontal limb in a
conifer; female builds a cup nest with grass, bark
strips, moss, lichens and spider silk; light buff to reddish brown, variably marked eggs are 17 x 13 mm;
female incubates 4–5 eggs for up to 13 days.

Did You Know?

The scientific name
coronata is Latin for
"crowned," referring to
this bird's yellow crown.

Look For

Foraging Yellow-rumped
Warblers frequently fly out
and snatch insects in mid-air
or hover and pick bugs off
leaves.

Common Yellowthroat

Geothlypis trichas

The bumblebee colours of the male Common Yellowthroat's black "mask" and yellow throat help to identify this skulking wetland resident. The cattail outposts from which he perches to sing his *witchety* song are strategically chosen, and he visits them in rotation, fiercely guarding his territory against the intrusion of other males. • The Common Yellowthroat is different than most wood-warblers, preferring marshlands and wet, overgrown meadows to forests. The female wears no "mask" and remains mostly hidden from view in thick vegetation where she tends to the family duties.

Other ID: dingy white belly.
Size: *L* 11–14 cm; *W* 17 cm.
Voice: song is a clear, oscillating *witchety witchety witchety-witch;* call is a sharp *tcheck* or *tchet.*
Status: *Coast:* common migrant and breeder on the inner south coast; rare migrant elsewhere. *Interior:* uncommon to common migrant and local breeder.
Habitat: cattail and bulrush marshes, sedge wetlands, riparian areas, beaver ponds and wet, overgrown meadows; sometimes forages in dry fields.

Similar Birds

Wilson's Warbler

Nashville Warbler

no "mask"

may show faint, white eye ring

olive green to olive brown upperparts

♀

broad, black "mask" with white upper border

♂

Nesting: near the ground in a small shrub or emergent vegetation; female builds an open cup nest of weeds, grasses, bark strips and mosses; brown-blotched, white eggs are 17 x 13 mm; female incubates 3–5 eggs for 12 days.

Did You Know?

The songs of Common Yellowthroats along with Marsh Wrens and Pied-billed Grebes, are well known in B.C.'s wetland ecosystems.

Look For

These birds appear in British Columbia mainly from May to September and sometimes remain in southern areas in winter.

Western Tanager
Piranga ludoviciana

The Western Tanager brings with it the colours of a tropical visitor on its short stay in our province. They raise a new generation of young and take advantage of the seasonal explosion of food in our forests before heading back to their exotic wintering grounds in Mexico and Central America.
• Despite the male's stunning plumage, the Western Tanager might take some patience to spot. His song can also be a challenge to recognize. It closely parallels the robin's tune, but the Western Tanager sings it with what sounds like a sore throat.

Other ID: *Breeding male:* black back, wings and tail. *Breeding female:* lighter underparts; darker upperparts.
Size: *L* 18 cm; *W* 29 cm.
Voice: call is a hiccupy *pit-a-tik. Male:* song is hoarse and robinlike: *hurry, scurry, scurry, hurry.*
Status: *Coast:* uncommon to common migrant and breeder on the inner south coast; rare to uncommon migrant elsewhere. *Interior:* uncommon to common migrant and breeder in the south; rare migrant and summer visitor in the northeast.
Habitat: mature coniferous forests, especially Douglas-fir or mixedwood forests and trembling aspen and poplar woodlands.

Similar Birds

Baltimore Oriole   Bullock's Oriole

olive green
overall

♀

red forehead or
entire head (variable)

light-coloured
bill

faint wing
bars

♂

yellow underparts
and wing bars

breeding

Nesting: on a horizontal branch or fork in a
conifer, well out from the trunk; cup nest is loosely
built of twigs, grasses and other plant materials
and lined with finer vegetation; brown spotted,
light blue or greenish eggs are 23 x 17 mm;
female incubates 4 eggs for 13–14 days.

Did You Know?

"Tanager" is derived from
tangara, the Tupi Indian
name for this group of
birds in the Amazon Basin.

Look For

The male Western Tanager
spends long periods of time
singing from the same perch.
Fruit-bearing trees and shrubs
are especially favoured in
migration.

Spotted Towhee

Pipilo maculatus

Do not be disappointed if the racoon or skunk you were expecting to see at close range turns out to be a bird not much larger than a sparrow. The Spotted Towhee is capable of quite a ruckus when it forages in loose leaf litter, scraping with both feet. • Although a confident bird, never hesitating to scold the family cat, Spotted Towhees can also be shy. They need some coaxing if you want to lure them into the open, and they tend to make themselves scarce in a crowded park of people.

Other ID: black wings and tail; white spotting on wings and back; white outer tail corners; white breast and belly; buffy undertail.

Size: *L* 18–21 cm; *W* 26 cm.

Voice: song is *here here here PLEASE;* distinctive call is a buzzy trill.

Status: *Coast:* common breeding resident on inner south coast, uncommon elsewhere on Vancouver I. *Interior:* common summer visitor and breeder in the south.

Habitat: brushy hedgerows and woods with dense understorey; overgrown bushy fields and hillsides; frequently at feeders, especially in winter.

Similar Birds

Dark-eyed Junco (p. 166)

Look For

The Spotted Towhee especially likes tangled thickets and overgrown gardens with blackberries and other small fruits.

black "hood" and back

red eyes

dark, conical bill

dark rufous sides and flanks

♂

Nesting: low in a shrub or in a depression on the ground; cup of leaves, bark and rootlets is lined with fine grasses and hair; brown-spotted, white eggs are 24 x 18 mm; pair incubates 3–4 eggs for 12–13 days.

Did You Know?

Until recently, the Spotted Towhee was grouped together with the Eastern Towhee as a single species called the "Rufous-sided Towhee." The Spotted is more commonly found in the western part of North America.

Chipping Sparrow
Spizella passerina

Though you may spot the relatively tame Chipping Sparrow singing from a high perch, it commonly nests at eye level, so you can easily watch its breeding and nest-building rituals. You can take part in the building of this bird's nest by leaving samples of your pet's hair—or your own—around your backyard. • This bird shares a very similar song with the Dark-eyed Junco and Orange-crowned Warbler. Listen for a slightly faster, drier and less musical series of notes to identify the Chipping Sparrow.

Other ID: *Nonbreeding:* paler crown with dark streaks; brown "eyebrow" and "cheek"; pale lower mandible.
Size: *L* 13–15 cm; *W* 21 cm.
Voice: song is a rapid, dry trill of *chip* notes; call is a high-pitched *chip*.
Status: *Coast:* uncommon migrant and breeder on inner south coast; rare migrant elsewhere. *Interior:* common migrant and breeder.
Habitat: open conifers or mixed woodland edges; subalpine thickets; yards and gardens with tree and shrub borders.

Similar Birds

American Tree Sparrow

Brewer's Sparrow

Clay-colored Sparrow

prominent rufous "cap"

white "eyebrow"

black eye line

mottled brown
upperparts

breeding

Nesting: usually at midlevel in a small coniferous tree; female builds a cup nest of grasses and rootlets lined with hair; pale blue eggs are 18 x 13 mm; female incubates 4 eggs for 11–12 days.

Did You Know?

The Chipping Sparrow is the most common and widely distributed migrating sparrow in North America.

Look For

Chipping Sparrows may visit feeders, but are more often seen foraging on weedy lawns for the seeds of grasses, dandelions and clovers.

Song Sparrow
Melospiza melodia

Although its plumage is unremarkable, the appropriately named Song Sparrow is among the great singers of the bird world. By the time a young male Song Sparrow is a few months old, he has created a courtship tune of his own, having learned the basics of melody and rhythm from his father and male rivals. • Each season, pairs of Song Sparrows will raise as many as three families. The presence of a well-stocked backyard feeder may be a fair trade for a sweet song in the dead of winter.

Other ID: mottled brown upperparts.
Size: *L* 14–18 cm; *W* 20 cm.
Voice: song is 1–4 introductory notes, such as *sweet sweet sweet*, followed by buzzy *towee*, then a short, descending trill; call is short *tsip* or *tchep*.
Status: *Coast:* common breeding resident. *Interior:* common breeding resident in the south; uncommon to common migrant and breeder farther north.
Habitat: beaches, lakeshores and riparian thickets, forest openings, shrubby pastures and residential gardens, all often near water.

Similar Birds

Lincoln's Sparrow

Fox Sparrow

Savannah Sparrow

dark crown with pale central stripe

white jaw line

dark "moustache" stripes

heavy brown streaks converge at central breast spot

Nesting: usually on the ground or in a low shrub; female builds an open cup nest of grasses, weeds and bark strips; brown-blotched, greenish white eggs are 22 x 17 mm; female incubates 3–5 eggs for 12–14 days.

Did You Know?

Though female songbirds are not usually vocal, the female Song Sparrow will occasionally sing a tune of her own.

Look For

The Song Sparrow pumps its long, rounded tail in flight.

Dark-eyed Junco

Junco hyemalis hyemalis ("Slate-colored")
Junco hyemalis oreganus ("Oregon")

You might spot this sparrow picking at the scraps underneath your backyard feeder; it prefers to avoid the crowds of noshing chickadees, nuthatches and jays. • In 1973, the American Ornithologists' Union grouped junco species, all of which interbreed where their ranges meet, into a single species called the Dark-eyed Junco. • These ground-feeding sparrows brave the worst of winter in lowlands across the province. In severe weather, they fold their feet under their bodies and fluff out their feathers on the snow like a quilt.

Other ID: *Female:* brown overall.
Size: L 14–17 cm; W 23 cm.
Voice: song is a long, dry trill; call is a smacking *chip* note, often given in series.
Status: *Coast:* abundant migrant and common year-round resident. *Interior:* abundant migrant; common year-round resident in the south; mostly breeds in the north.
Habitat: *Breeding:* coniferous and mixed forests; shrubby, regenerating areas. *In migration* and *winter:* shrubby woodland borders, backyard feeders.

Similar Birds

Spotted Towhee
(p. 160)

Look For

The Dark-eyed Junco flashes its distinctive white outer tail feathers when it rushes for cover after being flushed.

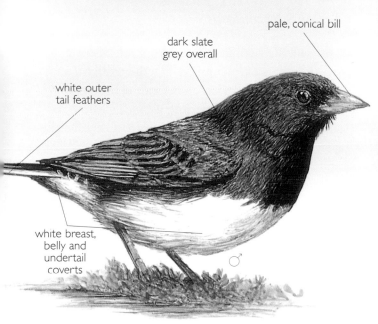

pale, conical bill

dark slate
grey overall

white outer
tail feathers

white breast,
belly and
undertail
coverts

♂

"Slate-colored Junco"

Nesting: on the ground, usually concealed; female builds a cup nest of twigs, grasses, bark shreds and mosses; brown-marked, whitish to bluish eggs are 19 x 14 mm; female incubates 3–5 eggs for 12–13 days.

Did You Know?

The subspecies of Juncos that were combined to make the "Dark-eyed Junco" are the Slate-colored Junco, the Oregon Junco, the Pink-sided Junco and the Northern Rockies Junco. In B.C., the "Oregon" form lives in the south and the "Slate-colored" resides in the north.

Red-winged Blackbird
Agelaius phoeniceus

The male Red-winged Blackbird wears his bright red shoulders like armour—together with his short, raspy song, they are key in defending his territory from rivals. In field experiments, males whose red shoulders were painted black soon lost their territories. • Red-winged Blackbirds breed north to Alaska and some retreat to the southwestern mainland of B.C. for the winter. It isn't hard to spot the polygynous males perched atop cattails in roadside ditches and wetlands, but the cryptically coloured females usually remain inconspicuous on their nests.

Other ID: *Female:* faint, red shoulder patch.
Size: L 18–24 cm; W 33 cm.
Voice: song is a loud, raspy *konk-a-ree* or *ogle-reeeee;* calls include a harsh *check* and high *tseert;* female gives a loud *che-che-che chee chee chee.*
Status: *Coast:* abundant year-round resident on inner south coast; rare to uncommon migrant and summer visitor elsewhere. *Interior:* common year-round resident in the south-central region; uncommon to common migrant and breeder elsewhere.
Habitat: cattail marshes, swamps, wet meadows and brushy ditches, croplands and lakeshore shrubs.

Similar Birds

Rusty Blackbird

Brown-headed Cowbird (p. 174)

Brewer's Blackbird

red shoulder
patch edged
in yellow

pale
"eyebrow"

black
overall

mottled
brown
upperparts

heavily
streaked
underparts

♂

♀

Nesting: mostly colonial; in cattails or shoreline bushes; female builds an open cup nest of dried cattail leaves lined with fine grasses; darkly marked, pale blue green eggs are 25 x 18 mm; female incubates 3–4 eggs for 10–12 days.

Did You Know?

Some scientists believe that the Red-winged Blackbird is the most abundant bird of any species in North America.

Look For

The female Red-winged Blackbird resembles a large sparrow with streaky plumage and a pale eye stripe.

Western Meadowlark
Sturnella neglecta

A lack of its recognition as a separate species earned the Western Meadowlark the scientific name, *neglecta.* Distinguishing this bird from its eastern twin might be one of the more challenging identification tests of birding. With the same cryptic outfit and grassland residence, there is little to tell them apart. Western Meadowlarks do, however, prefer drier, more barren grasslands compared with the wetter habitat of the Eastern, but their differing songs is probably the most accurate way to distinguish them.

Other ID: long, pinkish legs; yellow lores; pale "eyebrow" and median crown stripe; yellow on throat extends onto lower "cheek."
Size: *L* 23–24 cm; *W* 35–38 cm.
Voice: song is rich, melodic series of bubbly, flutelike notes; calls include a low, loud *chuck* or *chup,* a rattling flight call or a few clear whistled notes.
Status: *Coast:* rare to uncommon breeding resident in inner south coast; rare migrant elsewhere. *Interior:* common migrant and breeder in the south-central region; rare migrant and breeder in southern Peace River; rare elsewhere.
Habitat: open country, including grassland, pastures, rangeland and weedy farm fields.

Similar Birds

Dickcissel

Look For

Watch for the Western Meadowlark's courtship dance. Potential partners face each other, raise their bills high in the air and perform a grassland ballet.

long, sharp bill

mottled brown
upperparts

white outer
tail feathers

yellow underparts

short,
wide tail

dark streaking on
white sides and flanks

Nesting: a depression or scrape on the ground in dense grasses; domed grass nest with side entrance is woven into surrounding vegetation; brown and purple spotted, white eggs are 28 x 21 mm; female incubates 3–7 eggs for 13–15 days.

Did You Know?

Eastern Meadowlarks and Western Meadowlarks may occasionally interbreed where their ranges overlap, but their offspring are infertile.

Yellow-headed Blackbird

Xanthocephalus xanthocephalus

You might be taken aback by the pitiful grinding sound that is produced when the male Yellow-headed Blackbird arches his dazzling golden head backward to sing his nonmuscial series of grating notes. • Crafty Yellow-headed Blackbirds are strategic in sharing their soggy habitat with the smaller Red-winged Blackbirds—Yellow-heads tend to take over the more protected centre of the wetland and Red-winged Blackbirds prefer the outskirts.

Other ID: *Male:* black lores; long tail. *Female:* yellow breast and throat.
Size: L 20–28 cm; W 33–38 cm.
Voice: song is a strained, metallic grating note with a descending buzz; call is a deep *krrt* or *ktuk;* low quacks and liquidy clucks in breeding season.
Status: *Coast:* uncommon migrant and local breeder in the Lower Mainland; rare elsewhere. *Interior:* common migrant and abundant, local breeder in the south-central region; uncommon in Peace River; rare elsewhere.
Habitat: marshes, shallow lakes, lakeshores and rivers where bulrushes dominate.

Similar Birds

Rusty Blackbird

Brewer's Blackbird

dusky brown overall

yellow "eyebrow"

♀

♂

yellow head and breast

white wing patches

black body

Nesting: colonial; female builds a deep basket of aquatic plants, lined with dry grasses, woven into surrounding vegetation over water; grey- or brown-marked, pale green to grey eggs are 26 x 18 mm; female incubates 4 eggs for 11–13 days.

Did You Know?

The Yellow-headed Blackbird requires a hemi-marsh with a 50:50 ratio of emergent vegetation and open water.

Look For

These blackbirds often nest in small colonies of about 30 pairs. The gathered yellow heads of the males turn fields to the colour of mustard.

Brown-headed Cowbird
Molothrus ater

Brown-headed Cowbirds are best described as pests. These nomads historically followed bison herds across the prairies and do not build their own nests. Instead, they lay their eggs in other birds' nests; unsuspecting parents are left to incubate cowbird eggs and raise the aggressive young. Sparrows, warblers, vireos and thrushes are among the most affected. Increased livestock farming and fragmentation of forests has encouraged the expansion of the cowbird's range and it now parasitizes more than 140 bird species.

Other ID: *Female:* pale throat.
Size: *L* 15–20 cm; *W* 30 cm.
Voice: song is a high, liquidy gurgle: *glug-ahl-whee* or *bubbloozeee;* call is a squeaky, high-pitched *seep, psee* or *wee-tse-tse* or fast, chipping *ch-ch-ch-ch-ch-ch.*
Status: *Coast:* uncommon to common breeder in the south; rare to uncommon migrant in the north. *Interior:* uncommon to common breeder in the south; uncommon in the north.
Habitat: fields, woodland edges, transmission corridors, landfills, parks and areas near cattle.

Similar Birds

Brewer's Blackbird   Rusty Blackbird   Common Grackle

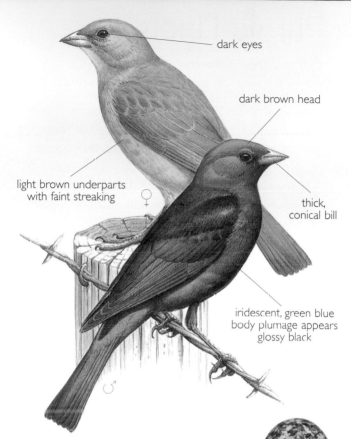

dark eyes

dark brown head

light brown underparts
with faint streaking ♀

thick,
conical bill

iridescent, green blue
body plumage appears
glossy black

♂

Nesting: does not build a nest; female may lay up
to 40 eggs a season in the nests of other birds,
usually 1 egg per nest; brown-speckled, whitish
eggs are 21 x 16 mm; eggs hatch after 10–13 days.

Did You Know?

In his courtship display,
the male points his bill
upward, fans his tail and
wings and utters a loud
squeek, but no pair bond
is formed.

Look For

When cowbirds feed in
flocks, they hold their back
ends high, with their tails
sticking straight up in the air.

Purple Finch
Carpodacus purpureus

Despite this bird's name, the male Purple Finch's stunning plumage is more raspberry red than purple. Its musical *pik* call note is given frequently and is a good way to know if this finch is nearby.
• In breeding season, the male dances around the female, beating his wings rapidly until they become a blur as he gracefully lifts into the air.

Other ID: *Male:* brown and red streaking on back and flanks; red rump; notched tail.
Size: *L* 13–15 cm; *W* 25 cm.
Voice: song is a bubbly, continuous warble; call is a single metallic *pik*.
Status: *Coast:* uncommon year-round in the inner coast; rare elsewhere. *Interior:* rare migrant and summer visitor in the south; uncommon migrant and summer visitor from the Cariboo northward.
Habitat: *Breeding:* coniferous and mixed hardwood forests. *In migration* and *winter:* mixed coniferous and deciduous forests, shrubby open areas and feeders.

Similar Birds

House Finch

Red Crossbill

Cassin's Finch

grey brown upperparts with whitish streaks

dark brown "cheek" and "jawline"

pale bill

heavily streaked underparts

♀

♂

reddish brown "cheek"

pale, unstreaked underparts

Nesting: on a conifer branch, far from the trunk; female builds a cup nest of twigs, grasses and rootlets; darkly marked, pale-greenish blue eggs are 20 x 15 mm; female incubates 4–5 eggs for 13 days.

Did You Know?

A raised, table-style feeding station and nearby tree cover are sure to attract Purple Finches, and may keep a small flock in your area over winter.

Look For

The Purple Finch has more pronounced head markings than the House Finch and is more common in winter than the similar, occasionally visiting, Common Redpoll.

Pine Siskin
Carduelis pinus

When it rains siskins, it pours. Pine Siskins fluctuate in abundance both seasonally and in accordance with availability of favoured food sources. Pine Siskins are most numerous during invasive appearances, which take place chiefly in the fall, winter, and spring. They consume niger thistle seeds in great quantities, and a few dozen of these birds lingering at your feeding station can necessitate its daily restocking. It is important to maintain dry seed—rain-soaked seed can rot, causing salmonella outbreaks which may incapacitate or kill feeder-dependent birds.

ID: *Immature:* dull white in the wings and tail.
Size: L 11–13 cm; W 22–23 cm.
Voice: song is variable; flight call is an exhuberant *shree!*; feeding flocks give a rising, extended *shhrreee* with a hectic *chut-chut-chut*.
Status: *Coast:* irregularly common to abundant year-round. *Interior:* irruptive year-round; irregularly uncommon migrant and breeder in the north.
Habitat: *Breeding:* coniferous and hardwood forests; exotic plantations. *In migration* and *winter:* any natural or human-influenced habitat.

Similar Birds

American Goldfinch (p. 180)

Common Redpoll

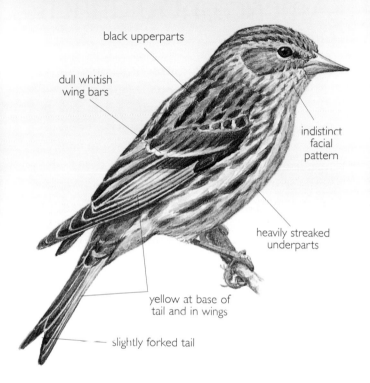

black upperparts

dull whitish
wing bars

indistinct
facial
pattern

heavily streaked
underparts

yellow at base of
tail and in wings

slightly forked tail

Nesting: loosely communal; often on an outer
branch in a conifer; nest is woven with grasses
and small roots and lined with fur and feathers;
greenish-blue eggs, spotted with purplish-black, are
17 x 12 mm; female incubates 3–4 eggs for 13 days.

Did You Know?

Prior to recent taxonomic
changes, the Pine Siskin
had the catchy, easy to
remember scientific name,
Spinus pinus.

Look For

Once you recognize the distinctive chattering of these
gregarious finches, look for
a flurry of activity and flashes
of yellow in treetops.

American Goldfinch
Carduelis tristis

Like tiny rays of sunshine, American Goldfinches cheerily flutter over weedy fields, gardens and along roadsides. It is hard to miss their jubilant call and their distinctive, undulating flight style. • Because these acrobatic birds regularly feed while hanging upside down, finch feeders have been designed with the seed opening below the perch. These feeders discourage more aggressive House Sparrows from stealing the seeds. Use niger or millet seeds to attract American Goldfinches to your bird feeder.

Other ID: *Breeding male:* orange bill and legs; white rump and undertail coverts. *Female:* yellow throat and breast; yellow green belly. *Nonbreeding male:* olive brown back; yellow-tinged head; grey underparts.
Size: *L* 11–14 cm; *W* 23 cm.
Voice: song is a long, varied series of trills, twitters, warbles and hissing notes; calls include *po-ta-to-chip* or *per-chic-or-ee* (often delivered in flight) and a whistled *dear-me, see-me.*
Status: *Coast:* common migrant and resident on Vancouver I. and Lower Mainland southward. *Interior:* common winter resident in south-central B.C.; migrant and breeder in southeast.
Habitat: weedy fields, woodland edges, meadows, riparian areas, parks and gardens.

Similar Birds

Evening Grosbeak

Wilson's Warbler

yellow green
upperparts

black "cap"
extends onto
forehead

♀

♂

black wings and
tail with white
wing bars

Nesting: in the fork of a deciduous tree; compact cup nest of plant fibres, grass and spider silk;
pale blue to greenish blue eggs are 16 x 12 mm;
female incubates 4–6 eggs for about 12–14 days.

Did You Know?

These birds nest in late
summer to ensure that
there is a dependable
source of seeds from this-
tles and dandelions to
feed their young.

Look For

American Goldfinches delight
in perching on late-summer
thistle heads or poking
through dandelion patches
in search of seeds.

House Sparrow
Passer domesticus

A black "mask" and "bib" adorn the male of this adaptive and aggressive species. The House Sparrow's tendency to usurp territory that can lead to a local decline in native bird numbers. This sparrow will even help itself to the convenience of another bird's home, such as a bluebird or Cliff Swallow nest or a Purple Martin house. • This abundant and conspicuous bird was introduced to North America in the 1850s as part of a plan to control the insects that were damaging grain and cereal crops. As it turns out, these birds are largely vegetarian!

Other ID: *Breeding male:* dark, mottled upperparts; white wing bar. *Female:* indistinct facial patterns; greyish unstreaked underparts.
Size: L 14–17 cm; W 24 cm.
Voice: song is a plain, familiar *cheep-cheep-cheep-cheep;* call is a short *chill-up.*
Status: *Coast:* locally common, year-round breeding resident in the inner coast. *Interior:* locally common year-round northward to Smithers and in the south Peace River region.
Habitat: townsites, urban and suburban areas, farmyards and agricultural areas, railway yards and industrial areas.

Similar Birds

Harris's Sparrow

Purple Finch (p. 176)

buffy "eyebrow"

chestnut nape extends to eye

black lores and "bib"

light grey "cheek"

♀

♂

breeding

Nesting: often communal; in a human-made structure, ornamental shrub or nest box; pair builds a large dome nest of grasses, twigs and plant fibres; grey-speckled, white to greenish eggs are 23 x 16 mm; pair incubates 4–6 eggs for 10–13 days.

Did You Know?

House Sparrows are not closely related to other North American sparrows, but belong to the family of Old World Sparrows or "Weaver Finches."

Look For

In spring, House Sparrows feast on the buds of fruit trees. In winter, these birds flock together around barns in rural areas and at city garbage dumps.

Glossary

accipiter: a forest hawk (genus *Accipiter*), characterized by a long tail and short, rounded wings; feeds mostly on birds.

brood: *n.* a family of young from one hatching; *v.* to incubate the eggs.

brood parasite: a bird that lays its eggs in other birds' nests.

buteo: a high-soaring hawk (genus *Buteo*), characterized by broad wings and a short, wide tail; feeds mostly on small mammals and other land animals.

cere: on birds of prey, a fleshy area at the base of the bill that contains the nostrils.

clutch: the number of eggs laid by the female at one time.

dabbling: a foraging technique used by some ducks, in which the head and neck are submerged but the body and tail remain on the water's surface; dabbling ducks can usually walk easily on land, can take off without running and have brightly coloured speculums.

"eclipse" plumage: a cryptic plumage, similar to that of females, worn by some male ducks in autumn when they moult their flight feathers and consequently are unable to fly.

flushing: when frightened birds explode into flight in response to a disturbance.

flycatching: a feeding behaviour in which the bird leaves a perch, snatches an insect in mid-air and returns to the same perch; also known as "hawking" or "sallying."

pelagic: refers to birds that inhabit the ocean very far from land.

precocial: a bird that is relatively well developed at hatching; precocial birds usually have open eyes, extensive down and are fairly mobile.

riparian: refers to habitat along riverbanks.

sexual dimorphism: a difference in plumage, size, or other characteristics between males and females of the same species.

speculum: a brightly coloured patch on the mid-wing of many dabbling ducks.

stage: to gather in one place during migration, or when birds are flightless or partially flightless during moulting.

stoop: a steep dive through the air, usually performed by birds of prey while foraging or during courtship displays.

Checklist

The following checklist contains 363 regularly occuring species of birds that are seen in British Columbia. It is based on the Checklist of British Columbia Birds, compiled by Wayne Campbell *et al.* (2005). Species are grouped by family and listed in taxonomic order in accordance with the A.O.U. *Check-list of North American Birds* (7th ed.) and its supplements.

Waterfowl
❏ Greater White-fronted Goose
❏ Emperor Goose
❏ Snow Goose
❏ Brant
❏ Cackling Goose
❏ Canada Goose
❏ Mute Swan
❏ Trumpeter Swan
❏ Tundra Swan
❏ Wood Duck
❏ Mandarin Duck
❏ Gadwall
❏ Eurasian Wigeon
❏ American Wigeon
❏ American Black Duck
❏ Mallard
❏ Blue-winged Teal
❏ Cinnamon Teal
❏ Northern Shoveler
❏ Northern Pintail
❏ Green-winged Teal
❏ Canvasback
❏ Redhead
❏ Ring-necked Duck
❏ Tufted Duck
❏ Greater Scaup
❏ Lesser Scaup
❏ Harlequin Duck
❏ Surf Scoter
❏ White-winged Scoter
❏ Black Scoter
❏ Long-tailed Duck
❏ Bufflehead
❏ Common Goldeneye
❏ Barrow's Goldeneye
❏ Hooded Merganser
❏ Common Merganser
❏ Red-breasted Merganser
❏ Ruddy Duck

Grouse & Allies
❏ Chukar
❏ Gray Partridge
❏ Ring-necked Pheasant
❏ Ruffed Grouse
❏ Spruce Grouse
❏ Willow Ptarmigan
❏ Rock Ptarmigan
❏ White-tailed Ptarmigan
❏ Blue Grouse
❏ Sharp-tailed Grouse
❏ Wild Turkey

Quail
❏ California Quail

Loons
❏ Red-throated Loon
❏ Pacific Loon
❏ Common Loon
❏ Yellow-billed Loon

Grebes
❏ Pied-billed Grebe
❏ Horned Grebe
❏ Red-necked Grebe
❏ Eared Grebe
❏ Western Grebe
❏ Clark's Grebe

Albatrosses
❏ Laysan Albatross
❏ Black-footed Albatross

Shearwaters & Petrels
❏ Northern Fulmar
❏ Pink-footed Shearwater
❏ Flesh-footed Shearwater
❏ Buller's Shearwater
❏ Sooty Shearwater
❏ Short-tailed Shearwater
❏ Manx Shearwater

Storm-Petrels
❏ Fork-tailed Storm-Petrel
❏ Leach's Storm-Petrel

Pelicans
❏ American White Pelican
❏ Brown Pelican

Cormorants
❏ Brandt's Cormorant
❏ Double-crested Cormorant
❏ Pelagic Cormorant

Herons
❏ American Bittern
❏ Great Blue Heron
❏ Cattle Egret
❏ Green Heron
❏ Black-crowned Night-Heron

Vultures
❏ Turkey Vulture

Hawks & Eagles
❏ Osprey
❏ Bald Eagle
❏ Northern Harrier
❏ Sharp-shinned Hawk
❏ Cooper's Hawk
❏ Northern Goshawk
❏ Broad-winged Hawk
❏ Swainson's Hawk
❏ Red-tailed Hawk
❏ Rough-legged Hawk
❏ Golden Eagle

Falcons
❏ Crested Caracara
❏ American Kestrel
❏ Merlin
❏ Gyrfalcon
❏ Peregrine Falcon
❏ Prairie Falcon

Rails & Coots
❏ Virginia Rail
❏ Sora
❏ American Coot

Cranes
❏ Sandhill Crane

Plovers
❏ Black-bellied Plover
❏ American Golden-Plover
❏ Pacific Golden-Plover
❏ Semipalmated Plover
❏ Killdeer

Oystercatchers
❏ Black Oystercatcher

Stilts & Avocets
❏ American Avocet

Sandpipers & Allies
❏ Greater Yellowlegs
❏ Lesser Yellowlegs
❏ Solitary Sandpiper
❏ Wandering Tattler
❏ Spotted Sandpiper
❏ Upland Sandpiper
❏ Whimbrel
❏ Long-billed Curlew
❏ Hudsonian Godwit
❏ Marbled Godwit
❏ Ruddy Turnstone
❏ Black Turnstone
❏ Surfbird
❏ Red Knot
❏ Sanderling
❏ Semipalmated Sandpiper
❏ Western Sandpiper
❏ Least Sandpiper
❏ White-rumped Sandpiper
❏ Baird's Sandpiper
❏ Pectoral Sandpiper
❏ Sharp-tailed Sandpiper
❏ Rock Sandpiper
❏ Dunlin
❏ Stilt Sandpiper
❏ Buff-breasted Sandpiper
❏ Short-billed Dowitcher
❏ Long-billed Dowitcher
❏ Common Snipe
❏ Wilson's Phalarope
❏ Red-necked Phalarope
❏ Red Phalarope

Gulls & Allies
❏ Pomarine Jaeger
❏ Parasitic Jaeger
❏ Long-tailed Jaeger
❏ Franklin's Gull
❏ Bonaparte's Gull
❏ Heermann's Gull
❏ Mew Gull
❏ Ring-billed Gull
❏ California Gull
❏ Herring Gull
❏ Thayer's Gull
❏ Western Gull

❏ Glaucous-winged Gull
❏ Glaucous Gull
❏ Sabine's Gull
❏ Black-legged Kittiwake
❏ Caspian Tern
❏ Common Tern
❏ Arctic Tern
❏ Forster's Tern
❏ Black Tern

Murres, Auks, Puffins

❏ Common Murre
❏ Thick-billed Murre
❏ Pigeon Guillemot
❏ Marbled Murrelet
❏ Ancient Murrelet
❏ Cassin's Auklet
❏ Rhinoceros Auklet
❏ Horned Puffin
❏ Tufted Puffin

Pigeons & Doves

❏ Rock Pigeon
❏ Band-tailed Pigeon
❏ Mourning Dove

Barn Owls

❏ Barn Owl

Owls

❏ Flammulated Owl
❏ Western Screech-Owl
❏ Great Horned Owl
❏ Snowy Owl
❏ Northern Hawk Owl
❏ Northern Pygmy-Owl
❏ Burrowing Owl
❏ Spotted Owl
❏ Barred Owl
❏ Great Gray Owl
❏ Long-eared Owl
❏ Short-eared Owl
❏ Boreal Owl
❏ Northern Saw-whet Owl

Nightjars

❏ Common Nighthawk
❏ Common Poorwill

Swifts

❏ Black Swift
❏ Vaux's Swift
❏ White-throated Swift

Hummingbirds

❏ Black-chinned Hummingbird
❏ Anna's Hummingbird
❏ Calliope Hummingbird
❏ Rufous Hummingbird

Kingfishers

❏ Belted Kingfisher

Woodpeckers

❏ Lewis's Woodpecker
❏ Yellow-bellied Sapsucker
❏ Red-naped Sapsucker
❏ Red-breasted Sapsucker
❏ Williamson's Sapsucker
❏ Downy Woodpecker
❏ Hairy Woodpecker
❏ White-headed Woodpecker
❏ American Three-toed
  Woodpecker
❏ Black-backed Woodpecker
❏ Northern Flicker
❏ Pileated Woodpecker

Flycatchers

❏ Olive-sided Flycatcher
❏ Western Wood-Pewee
❏ Yellow-bellied Flycatcher
❏ Alder Flycatcher
❏ Willow Flycatcher
❏ Least Flycatcher
❏ Hammond's Flycatcher
❏ Gray Flycatcher
❏ Dusky Flycatcher
❏ Pacific-slope Flycatcher
❏ Eastern Phoebe
❏ Say's Phoebe
❏ Western Kingbird
❏ Eastern Kingbird

Shrikes

❏ Loggerhead Shrike
❏ Northern Shrike

Vireos

❏ Cassin's Vireo
❏ Blue-headed Vireo
❏ Hutton's Vireo
❏ Warbling Vireo
❏ Philadelphia Vireo
❏ Red-eyed Vireo

Jays & Crows

❏ Gray Jay
❏ Steller's Jay
❏ Blue Jay
❏ Clark's Nutcracker

- ❏ Black-billed Magpie
- ❏ American Crow
- ❏ Northwestern Crow
- ❏ Common Raven

Larks
- ❏ Sky Lark
- ❏ Horned Lark

Swallows
- ❏ Purple Martin
- ❏ Tree Swallow
- ❏ Violet-green Swallow
- ❏ Northern Rough-winged Swallow
- ❏ Bank Swallow
- ❏ Cliff Swallow
- ❏ Barn Swallow

Chickadees
- ❏ Black-capped Chickadee
- ❏ Mountain Chickadee
- ❏ Chestnut-backed Chickadee
- ❏ Boreal Chickadee

Bushtits
- ❏ Bushtit

Nuthatches
- ❏ Red-breasted Nuthatch
- ❏ White-breasted Nuthatch
- ❏ Pygmy Nuthatch

Creepers
- ❏ Brown Creeper

Wrens
- ❏ Rock Wren
- ❏ Canyon Wren
- ❏ Bewick's Wren
- ❏ House Wren
- ❏ Winter Wren
- ❏ Marsh Wren

Dippers
- ❏ American Dipper

Kinglets
- ❏ Golden-crowned Kinglet
- ❏ Ruby-crowned Kinglet

Bluebirds & Thrushes
- ❏ Western Bluebird
- ❏ Mountain Bluebird
- ❏ Townsend's Solitaire
- ❏ Veery
- ❏ Gray-cheeked Thrush
- ❏ Swainson's Thrush

- ❏ Hermit Thrush
- ❏ American Robin
- ❏ Varied Thrush

Mimics & Thrashers
- ❏ Gray Catbird
- ❏ Northern Mockingbird
- ❏ Sage Thrasher

Starlings
- ❏ European Starling

Pipits
- ❏ Gray Wagtail
- ❏ American Pipit

Waxwings
- ❏ Bohemian Waxwing
- ❏ Cedar Waxwing

Wood-Warblers
- ❏ Tennessee Warbler
- ❏ Orange-crowned Warbler
- ❏ Nashville Warbler
- ❏ Yellow Warbler
- ❏ Magnolia Warbler
- ❏ Cape May Warbler
- ❏ Yellow-rumped Warbler
- ❏ Black-throated Gray Warbler
- ❏ Black-throated Green Warbler
- ❏ Townsend's Warbler
- ❏ Palm Warbler
- ❏ Bay-breasted Warbler
- ❏ Blackpoll Warbler
- ❏ Black-and-white Warbler
- ❏ American Redstart
- ❏ Ovenbird
- ❏ Northern Waterthrush
- ❏ Connecticut Warbler
- ❏ Mourning Warbler
- ❏ MacGillivray's Warbler
- ❏ Common Yellowthroat
- ❏ Wilson's Warbler
- ❏ Canada Warbler
- ❏ Yellow-breasted Chat

Tanagers
- ❏ Western Tanager

Sparrows & Allies
- ❏ Spotted Towhee
- ❏ American Tree Sparrow
- ❏ Chipping Sparrow
- ❏ Clay-colored Sparrow
- ❏ Timberline Sparrow
- ❏ Brewer's Sparrow

❏ Vesper Sparrow
❏ Lark Sparrow
❏ Savannah Sparrow
❏ Grasshopper Sparrow
❏ Le Conte's Sparrow
❏ Nelson's Sharp-tailed Sparrow
❏ Fox Sparrow
❏ Song Sparrow
❏ Lincoln's Sparrow
❏ Swamp Sparrow
❏ White-throated Sparrow
❏ Harris's Sparrow
❏ White-crowned Sparrow
❏ Golden-crowned Sparrow
❏ Dark-eyed Junco
❏ Lapland Longspur
❏ Smith's Longspur
❏ Snow Bunting

Grosbeaks & Buntings
❏ Rose-breasted Grosbeak
❏ Black-headed Grosbeak
❏ Lazuli Bunting

Blackbirds & Allies
❏ Bobolink
❏ Red-winged Blackbird

❏ Western Meadowlark
❏ Yellow-headed Blackbird
❏ Rusty Blackbird
❏ Brewer's Blackbird
❏ Common Grackle
❏ Brown-headed Cowbird
❏ Bullock's Oriole
❏ Baltimore Oriole

Finches
❏ Brambling
❏ Gray-crowned Rosy-Finch
❏ Pine Grosbeak
❏ Purple Finch
❏ Cassin's Finch
❏ House Finch
❏ Red Crossbill
❏ White-winged Crossbill
❏ Common Redpoll
❏ Hoary Redpoll
❏ Pine Siskin
❏ American Goldfinch
❏ Evening Grosbeak

Old World Sparrows
❏ House Sparrow

Select References

American Ornithologists' Union. 1998. *Check-list of North American Birds.* 7th ed. (and its supplements). American Ornithologists' Union, Washington, D.C.

Baron, Nancy and John Acorn. 1997. *Birds of Coastal British Columbia.* Lone Pine Publishing, Edmonton, Alberta.

Butler, Elaine. 1991. *Attracting Birds.* Lone Pine Publishing, Edmonton, Alberta.

Campbell, R.W., et al. 1990–2001. *The Birds of British Columbia.* Vols. 1–4. University of British Columbia Press, Vancouver.

Elphick, C., J.B. Dunning, Jr., and D.A. Sibley, eds. 2001. *National Audubon Society The Sibley Guide to Bird Life & Behavior.* Alfred A. Knopf, New York.

Roth, Sally. 1998. *Attracting Birds to Your Backyard 536 Ways to Turn Your Yard and Garden into a Haven for Your Favorite Birds.* Rodale Press, Inc. Emmaus, Pennsylvania.

Sibley, D.A. 2000. *National Audubon Society The Sibley Guide to Birds.* Alfred A. Knopf, New York.

Index

Rufous Hummingbird